STUDIES IN THE PERSON & WORK OF JESUS CHRIST

W. E. BEST

BAKER BOOK HOUSE
Grand Rapids, Michigan

ISBN: 0-8010-0644-9

Printed in the United States of America

PREFACE

I affectionately dedicate this book to my Christian friends with whom I have labored for many years. Their faithful support has enabled me to give myself wholly to the study and ministry of God's Word; and their hunger for spiritual food has been, second to the indwelling Spirit, a great challenge for the searching of hidden treasures. "Yea, if thou criest after knowledge, and liftest up thy voice for understanding; If thou seekest her as silver, and searchest for her as for hid treasures; Then shalt thou understand the fear of the Lord, and find the knowledge of God" (Prov. 2:3-5).

Christians are admonished to be ready always to give a reason for their hope. This work contains my bold, and I trust Scripturally wise, profession of my faith in the Person and Work of Jesus Christ. As a minister of the Gospel of Christ, I must not be guilty of sinful silence on the most important subject of Scripture, namely, the Impeccable Christ.

The purpose of this book is not to impress scholars, but to awaken and feed the elect of God. I am aware that this work, as well as all human productions, is subject to endless improvement; but my heart's desire and prayer to God is that the reader will be helped a little to have a greater appreciation for the Person and Work of the Impeccable Christ.

W. E. Best

CONTENTS

Introduction 4

The Eternal Son Of God.................................. 11

The Son Declares The Father 16

The Mystery Of Godliness 22

The Manifestation Of Godliness 28

The Incarnation 33

The Virgin Birth 38

Christ's Human Nature 43

Christ's Human Body 50

Christ's Human Soul 55

Christ's Human Growth 62

Christ's Baptism 68

Christ's Temptation 74

Christ's Impeccable Life 80

The God Approved Man 85

Christ's Prayer Life 90

The Drawing Power Of Christ 94

Christ's Discriminating Message 99

Christ's Miracles 107

Christ's Death 113

Christ's Headship 119

Christ's Kingship 126

INTRODUCTION

Much controversy exists over the Person of Jesus Christ. Christians affirm the truth that Jesus Christ *could not sin*. Common teaching among religionists is that Christ assumed man's imperfect nature which bears the consequences of sin and tendencies to temptation. This concept is expressed in the following words: "Jesus had the capacity to sin, but did not do so. If it were impossible for Jesus to do otherwise, his temptations were not real. He played a part which was a sham." This is a clear view of the heresy that is being taught.

The point of view that Christ *could sin* is designated by the idea of *peccability*, and the fact that *He could not sin* is expressed by the term *Impeccability*. To suggest the capability or possibility of sinning would disqualify Christ as Saviour, for a *peccable christ would mean a peccable god*.

Holiness is far more than the absence of sin; it is positive virtue. The advocates of peccability say, "Christ could have sinned, but He did not." To say that He could have sinned is to deny positive holiness. To deny positive holiness, therefore, is to deny the holy character of God. Holiness is *positive virtue* which has *neither room for nor interest in sin*. The Lord Jesus could not sin because the days of His flesh meant only addition of experience, not variation of character. Holy humanity was united to Deity in one indivisible Person—the Impeccable Christ. Jesus Christ cannot have more holiness because He is perfectly holy; He cannot have less holiness because He is unchangingly holy.

The favorite saying of some is, "Let us not say that Christ could not sin, but that *He did not*." This may satisfy those who merely profess Christianity, but not the possessors of Jesus Christ. The answer should not be left to those who *profess* Christ, but to those who *know* Him as Saviour and Lord. Satan attacks the Rock of the church, the Person of the Son of God (Matt. 16:18). His work, testimony, and death would be absolutely nothing to us if He were not God. Christ's Person supports His sacrifice; in that same sense, He is our Rock. Peter's confession embraced the Person of Christ, even while he was ignorant of His sacrifice. His confession was evidenced by the declaration, ". . . Thou art the Christ, the Son of the living God" (Matt. 16:16). His ignorance concerning Christ's sacrifice was demonstrated by the utterance, ". . . Be it (suffering) far from thee, Lord: this shall not be unto thee" (Matt. 16:22). Just to say that Christ did not sin is to deny the positive virtue of holiness.

There is no aspect of the *Impeccable Saviour's Person* that is not mysterious, but Christian ministers are the "stewards of the mysteries of God" (I Cor. 4:1). They must keep these "mysteries" from being corrupted by human philosophy and vain deceit (Col. 2:8). A false opinion concerning the Person of Christ cannot be condemned without showing the tragic end to which it leads. Christians cannot sit in silence while the blessed Person of Christ is being attacked. It has been said that a false system has for accomplice whoever spares it by silence. The guardianship of the glory of the Person of Christ forms the chief part of the Christian witness. This is emphasized by John, "Whosoever denieth the Son, the same hath not the Father: . . ." (I John 2:23).

A serious mistake is made in the study of Christology when the Person of Christ is made a faint *object* while His work is made the great *subject*. The work of God—*election, regeneration, calling, justification, sanctification, and glorification*—is crowned by making believers objects of grace. If Christians are objects of Christ's love and grace, should not the Person of Christ be the *object* of the saint's love and adoration? The Person of Christ, not *religion*, is the supreme requisite. Christ makes new creatures of us; therefore, He is changed from the center to the circumference. "Who his own self bare our sins in his own body on the tree . . . " (I Peter 2:24). "That I may know him, and the power of his resurrection, and the fellowship of his sufferings, being made comformable unto his death;" (Phil. 3:10). "My meditation of him shall be sweet: I will be glad in the Lord" (Ps. 104:34). ". . . greater is he that is in you, than he that is in the world" (I John 4:4). As Christians love His fellowship by the Spirit now, so they hope for His coming in Person. "Then we which are alive and remain shall be caught up together with them in the clouds, to meet the Lord in the air: and so shall we ever be with the Lord" (I Thess. 4:17). Formalities and superficialities cannot take the place of the Lord Jesus Christ.

Christians believe the perfection of Christ's humanity. Holy humanity was united to Deity in one indivisible Person—the Impeccable Christ. The Son of God was as unstained in the virgin's womb as He was in the Father's bosom. He was as unspotted in the midst of the world's corruption as when He was the Father's delight before the creation of the world. He remained the Word when He became incarnate; therefore, He was unchanged in His Person. His Deity may be contemplated apart from His human nature because it existed from eternity. But His human nature is inseparable from Deity and cannot be thus contemplated. Christ has not forsaken His human nature since He ascended to heaven. It was neither defiled nor made Divine. Even though His human nature is exalted above the glory of angels and men, it is still a creature and must not be adored apart from Deity. Christ's taking of the human nature into union with the Divine nature involved no subtraction from the fulness of His Person. It was a nature prepared for Him and was in perfect harmony with His Divine nature.

One of the most startling expressions in all the Bible is Luke 1:35: "And the angel answered and said unto her, The Holy Ghost shall come upon thee, and the power of the Highest shall overshadow thee: therefore also that *holy thing* which shall be born of thee shall be called the Son of God." Human nature in all its stages is a wonderful thing in our universe of things. Human nature, however, is but a *thing* until a far more wonderful thing than itself is identified with it. The uniting of a nature to a person results in a human being. When the *Holy Thing* was conceived by the Holy Ghost in the womb of the virgin Mary, the Holy Thing *henceforth and forever* became united to the Son of God. If God is so holy that He cannot look upon sin (Hab. 1:13), then the Holy Thing He assumed was as holy as He is holy. He experienced at the incarnation a birth-holiness that we shall not experience until the glorification of our bodies. What is the true nature of His glorified body? How can we know since it does not yet appear what we ourselves shall be (I John 3:2)! But this one thing we know— His human nature began where we shall end.

The two natures of Christ are so united that if His human nature were able to sin, God could have sinned. In the mysterious constitution of Christ's Person, there are two distinct natures: the Divine, which is eternal, infinite, omnipotent, omniscient, and omnipresent; the human, which had a beginning, was finite, impotent, and earth bound. Jesus Christ was both infinite and finite—unlimited and limited—but *never Impeccable and peccable.*

Those who believe in peccability offer the following objections: "Would not the uniting of two natures in one person imply that when one nature sins the other also sins? What about Christ who was 'asleep on a pillow' (Mark 4:38)—or 'Christ died for our sins' (I Cor. 15:3)?" Are we to assert from these passages that God was asleep or that God died? To say that God was asleep or that God died is to deny the Scripture—"Behold, he that keepeth Israel shall neither slumber nor sleep" (Ps. 121:4), and ". . . Who (God) only hath immortality . . ." (I Tim. 6:15,16). What is the answer to this seeming dilemma? It is erroneous to say that God was asleep or that God died. It is equally false to claim that He who was asleep and died was not God. Both assertions would be false. The Scriptures teach that He who is the Son did assume flesh and blood (Heb. 2:14), that *through death* He might destroy him who has the power of death and bring life and immortality (II Tim. 1:10) to the elect. Immortality alone can go *through death* because it is not subject to death as we. The Person who died and slept was truly God; although, the Divine nature neither died nor slept any more than the soul of man dies or sleeps when breath leaves his body.

The Christian has no question concerning the kind of nature Jesus Christ assumed in the incarnation. If He had a nature that was capable of sinning, then the following would be true:

1. His mother was stained with the sin of unchastity.
2. He was the seed of the man and not the seed of the woman.
3. He was an illegitimate child.
4. He was a natural person; therefore, He was not the God-Man.
5. He was reduced to the level of a natural man.
6. He was not the second Person of the Trinity.
    (1) If He is not the second Person of the Godhead, then we are without the manifestation of God.
    (2) If there is no second Person of the Godhead, then there is no Trinity.
    (3) If there is no second Person, then there is no Mediator.
    (4) If there is no Mediator, then there is no Saviour.
    (5) If He is no Mediator, then Immortality has not been brought to light; and we stand on the edge of darkness, silence, and the grave.
7. He was not free from depravity and actual sin.

8. He would have had to pray, "Father forgive us," rather than, "Father forgive them" (Luke 23:34).

9. He had a depraved nature, and having a depraved nature could never have made the distinction, ". . . I ascend unto my Father, and your Father: and to my God and your God" (John 20:17).

10. He was peccable on earth; and if He were peccable on earth, He must have experienced some kind of conversion in His nature before He ascended to heaven.

The doctrine of Impeccability is questioned on the point of whether an Impeccable Person can be tempted. The questioner says, "If it were impossible for Jesus to do otherwise, his temptations were not real. He played the part of a sham." The answer to this foolish statement is simple to the spiritually enlightened mind. It is possible for a chihuahua dog to attack a lion, but it is impossible for the little dog to conquer the lion. God, absolutely considered, cannot be tempted (James 1:13). But Jesus Christ, *as man*, was tempted; *temptability does not imply susceptibility*. The incarnate Christ was attacked by Satan, but there was not the inner struggle of the two natures as in the case of Paul (Rom. 7:15-25). If the human nature had been contaminated by original sin as in mankind, then there would have been the possibility or capability of the incarnate Christ sinning. But such possibility is completely removed by the presence and power of the Holy Spirit in the conception, birth, and life of His human nature.

Although no human being is beyond the possibility of temptation, he may, by sovereign grace, be beyond the possibility of yielding. But this could never be said of our Saviour, for He never had a fallen nature with which to struggle. His human will was always subservient to the Divine will and could not act independently (John 8:28-30; I Cor. 11:3). All Christians agree that the Divine will of God cannot sin. Since this *quality* was the controlling factor in Christ's human will, the capability of sinning was eliminated. The complete subordination of Christ's will to the will of the Father removes any idea of conflict between the Divine and human natures of Christ. The conclusion, therefore, is not that Christ, the Impeccable Saviour, played the part of a hypocrite; but those who question His Impeccability are hypocrites because they pose as Christians, but deny the very foundation of Christianity. They seek to rob Christ of His Impeccable nature and reduce Him to such an one as themselves (Ps. 50:21).

Jesus Christ, the Impeccable Saviour, is the *infinite* sacrifice for sin. A peccable person is a finite person who could never make satisfaction to the infinite God, Who was injured by sin. Jesus Christ is the Impeccable Christ and therefore infinite. Infinite retribution cannot be borne by a finite creature, but Jesus Christ was able to bear the infinite punishment for sin. The infinity of Christ's Person abundantly compensates for the eternity of retribution, for sin is against the infinite God and therefore merits infinite punishment.

We must understand the terms *infinite* and *finite* in order to properly understand the Person and Work of Jesus Christ. When we say that God is *infinite,* the meaning is that He is unlimited, immeasurable, and incomprehensible. "Great is our Lord, and of great power: his understanding is infinite" (Ps. 147:5). "Hast thou not known? hast thou not heard, that the everlasting God, the Lord, the Creator of the ends of the earth, fainteth not, neither is weary? there is no searching of his understanding" (Is. 40:28). "O the depth of the riches both of the wisdom and knowledge of God! how unsearchable are his judgments, and his ways past finding out" (Rom. 11:33). He is not bounded by space; consequently, He is everywhere. He is not limited by time, so He is eternal. He is an independent Being, so all creatures depend on Him—He depends on none. God who is without bounds restricts everything. He set bounds to the sea (Job 38:10,11), the nation's habitation (Gen. 10:32), the heavens (Ps. 148:6), redemption (John 6:37), and wickedness (Rev. 17:17). God is infinite in all His attributes; therefore, we must learn to admire and adore where we cannot fathom. "Canst thou by searching find out God? canst thou find out the Almighty unto perfection? It is as high as heaven: what canst thou do? deeper than hell; what canst thou know? The measure thereof is longer than the earth, and broader than the sea" (Job 11:7-9). In heaven we shall see God clearly but not fully, for he is infinite. The revelation will be according to the size of our finite vessel, not according to the infinity of His nature. Man is bounded, limited, measurable, and searchable because he is finite. God is unbounded, unlimited, immeasurable, and unsearchable because He is infinite.

When enlightened by the Spirit of God, one will see how Jesus Christ—the infinite Son of God and the finite son of Mary—gives to us the One God-Man, the Mediator (Phil. 2:5-9; Acts 13:38; I Tim. 2:5). The title "Son of Man" could not be correctly applied, except prophetically (Dan. 7:13), until the incarnation. The expressions, "The Son of man which is in heaven" (John 3:13) and "What and if ye shall see the Son of man ascend up where he was before?" (John 6:62), are not inconsistent with this view. His Personality was not less connected with the human than with the Divine Nature. We do not mix the natures nor divide the Person. The Son of Man ascended where He was before as the Eternal Son of God. He is there now not only as the Son of God but as the Son of Man. The human nature enables Him to come in contact with the sinner; His Divine Nature gives merit to His work in the human nature.

Since it was man who sinned, justice requires that man give the satisfaction. It was imperative that the Saviour of man must, in the nature of man, satisfy the justice and wrath of God. "If one man sin against another, the judge shall judge him: but if a man sin against the Lord, who shall entreat for him?..." (I Sam. 2:25). Thus, the Scripture states that if one finite person sins against another finite person, the finite judge shall judge him; but if a finite person sins against the infinite God, who shall entreat for him? Finite man cannot entreat for the sinner, but the infinite Saviour can entreat for him. The doctrine of peccability stabs the very heart of Christ and His redemptive work.

THE ETERNAL SON OF GOD

The subject of Christ's Eternal Sonship yields in importance to none. If our thoughts on this subject are not God's thoughts, we will not only dishonor the Lord but will bring damnation to our own souls. The *thoughts of God* expressed in the Scriptures must be understood in their obvious significance.

Matthew records the first reference in the New Testament of the title "Son of God" (Matt. 16:16). Was Peter's confession due to the fact that Christ's mother was a virgin? This confession could be attested by "flesh and blood" on the recognized principles of evidence, but the Lord declared that His Eternal Sonship was a revelation from heaven. ". . . for flesh and blood hath not revealed it unto thee, but my Father which is in heaven" (Matt. 16:17). "Whosoever shall confess that Jesus is the Son of God, God dwelleth in him, and he in God" (I John 4:15).

We recognize that, in some sense, God may be described by the recognized principles of evidence (Ps. 19:1-11; Rom. 1:19,20), but the elect will not rest in descriptions of God. They demand a revelation of Him which must be given by Himself. This is sufficient proof that the Son of God, in the bosom of the Father, is a Divine Person. The revelation is not that He is a Son, or the Son born of a virgin, or the Son raised from the dead, though all these are truths concerning Him; it is *a revelation of Divine Sonship*. God is not known as the Father if the Son in the glory of the Godhead is not acknowledged. "Who is a liar but he that denieth that Jesus is the Christ? He is antichrist, that denieth the Father and the Son. Whosoever denieth the Son, the same hath not the Father: (but) he that acknowledgeth the Son hath the Father also" (I John 2:22,23).

Eternal Fatherhood demands Eternal Sonship. Those who deny the Deity of Christ argue, "If the Father begat the Son, He who was begotten had a beginning of existence. So there was a time when the Son did not exist, therefore, the begotten is inferior to the Begetter." There is *priority in the Godhead but not superiority*. If by inferiority is meant inferiority of *relation*, we admit the position that the Begotten is inferior to the Begetter. This is what Christ meant when He said, " . . . my Father is greater than I" (John 14:28). The Sender is greater than the Sent; therefore, the word *greater* has reference to *authority* and not character. As

11

Mediator in His state of humiliation, Christ was the Father's subordinate and servant. If by inferiority is meant inferiority of character, such a notion should be opposed as the greatest heresy ever devised by the depraved heart of man.

Filiation implies not only equality but *identity of nature.* The begotten must share the nature of his begetter. Where there is no communication of nature, there is no real generation. Our Saviour said, "I and my Father are one" (John 10:30). This is in the neuter which refers to *one substance,* not in the masculine which would refer to one person. Thus, the relation of Christ to the Father is an unanswerable argument for Christ's Deity. Among men the action of the future father is necessary to the production of his off-spring, but this is a consequence of human nature. Among Spiritual Beings, however, paternity and filiation are independent of all human necessity. The Father cannot in any sense exist before the Son in eternal generation. The relation of Father and Son is correlative and simultaneous. It is foolish to think of the eternal generation of the Son of God in terms of the human. The terms *Father* and *Son,* as used in the Godhead, imply co-equality in nature and co-eternality. Christ, therefore, never refers to the Father as His Lord. He says "My Father" (His by eternal generation) and "your Father" (ours by regeneration) in order to make the proper distinction between Deity and humanity.

The original Greek uses two words for *son*—one refers to *dignity of position* and the other to *relationship by birth.* The second is never used with reference to our Lord Jesus in His relationship to the Father. The Greek word translated *Son* in the expressions "Son of God" and "Son of Man" is not always used to designate the thought of being born of God or born of man, as many false teachers assume. The word often carries the thought of *being identified with.* The same word is used in the following passages: "children of the kingdom" (Matt. 13:38) ; "children of the bride-chamber" (Mark 2:19) ; "sons of thunder" (Mark 3:17) ; "children of this world" (Luke 16:8) ; "children of disobedience" (Eph. 2:2) ; "children of day, of light" (I Thess. 5:5).

The Son of God is the *only Begotten* of the Father (John 1:18). This "only begotten Son" is the same Person Who is designated the "Word" (John 1:1) ; and of Whom it is said, "He was made flesh and dwelt among us" (John 1:14). Those who object to the

Deity of Christ say, "If you have been 'begotten' then you are not 'eternal.' He cannot at the same time be the 'eternal Son' and the 'begotten Son.'" Person begets person and like begets like in human generation, but the Father begat the Son in eternal generation.

There is similarity between *begetting* and *speaking*. It can be said that they both *bring forth*. When we speak, we do so either *within* ourselves or *without* to others. Hebrews 1:1-6 portrays the glory of the Son of God in eternity and in time. "Who *being* the brightness of his glory, and the express image of his person . . ." declares His pre-existent and *eternal being. "Being made* so much better than the angels, . . . when he bringeth the first begotten into the world . . ." affirms His *manhood in time.* He always had Sonship as God, but by inheritance He obtained it as Man. Thus, He Who was eternally with the Father was brought forth in time (II Tim. 1:9-10).

Only begotten is a term which denotes *endearment* (John 1:18; 3:16). Isaac was not Abraham's *only* begotten (Heb. 11:17), for Ishmael was begotten by him too. Isaac was his *darling.* Why was Isaac his darling? The reason was he was the only begotten of Abraham by his wife Sarah. His other children were called "sons of the concubines" (Gen. 25:6). As Isaac was Abraham's darling, so Christ is God's darling. "Lord, how long wilt thou look on? rescue my soul from their destructions, my darling (Hebrew— my only one) from the lions" (Ps. 35:17). Thus Christ, as the Only Begotten of the Father, was the sole representative of the Being and Character of the One Who sent Him. He is of the same essence with the Father, yet He is a distinct Person from the Father. As the inherent splendor of the sun cannot exist without the inherent splendor from which it proceeds, so the Inherent Essence of God cannot live without its Manifested Essence, nor the Manifested Essence without the Inherent Essence from Whom He came.

The Son of God is the *Firstborn Son.* Firstborn is used to express the sovereignty, dignity, and prerogative of heirship of Christ's position among many brethren (Heb. 2:11-17). This term is used twice in the New Testament without referring to Christ (Heb. 11:28; 12:23), and seven times as His title. An examination of these references will reveal a three-fold use in the

New Testament: (1) Before all creation (Rom. 8:29; Col. 1:15)—eternal; (2) Firstborn of Mary (Matt. 1:25; Luke 2:7; Heb. 1:6)—His pre-incarnate and incarnate Person; (3) Firstborn of resurrection (Col. 1:18; Rev. 1:5)—first to be raised from the dead in resurrection life.

The Son of God is both the *Word* and *Son*. These two metaphors supplement and protect each other. To think of Christ merely as the *Word* might suggest an impersonal faculty in God. On the other hand, to think of Him only as the *Son* might limit us to the conception of a created being. When the two terms are combined, there is no room for either an impersonal faculty or a created being. The substance of John 1:1-18 is that He Who is the *logos* was *with God* and *was God*. Three great facts are presented in John 1:1; they are: (1) *When* the Word was—"in the beginning"; (2) *Where* the Word was—"with God"; and (3) *Who* the Word was—"God." First, the "Word was in the beginning." The sun, moon, and stars "were made" in the beginning, but the Word "was" in the beginning. Christ's existence and theirs differ radically. Had John said "before" the beginning, he would have presented eternity under the laws of time. This would have been as serious as to describe the infinite under the laws of the finite—as difficult as trying to measure the waters of the ocean by one drop in the kitchen sink. But John ascends, in spirit, far above time and space to the peaceful calm where God dwells. Second, "The Word was with God." This expression implies that He had an existence distinct from the Father. He was with Him. For example, He that is with me is not me. The Word was *at home* in the bosom of the Father; therefore, He never felt as an inferior with a superior but as a loving Son with a loving Father (Prov. 8:22-31). God took unspeakable delight in His Word, for in Him He beheld His own express image (Heb. 1:3). Third, "The Word was God." Sonship is, in truth, the great bulwark of the Deity of Christ. From eternity the Son of God sustained to the Father a relationship involving *identity of nature*. If in the Godhead there is no filiation, neither is there paternity; if there is not a Divine and Eternal Son, neither is there a Divine and Eternal Father. "Whosoever denieth the Son, the same hath not the Father . . ." (I John 2:23). ". . . He that honoureth not the Son honoureth not the Father which hath sent him" (John 5:23).

The eternity of our election depends on Eternal Sonship (Eph. 1:4; II Tim. 1:9). If He is not eternal, our election is not eternal, for we are elected in Him.

The integrity of our redemption depends on Eternal Sonship, for He is the Lamb that was "slain from the foundation of the world" (Rev. 13:8).

Our eternal preservation depends on Eternal Sonship. He said, "Because I live, ye shall live also" (John 14:19). Nothing can survive to eternity but that which came from eternity.

Our choice is between inferiority of *nature* and inferiority of *relation*. Christians believe that there is subordination in the Trinity, but strongly deny inferiority of nature in the Godhead. To the Christian, there is no alternative but the *good confession* (I Tim. 6:13) of an eternal and Divine relation between the Subsistences of the Trinity. The Father, as God, begets; the Son, as God, is begotten; the Holy Spirit, as God, proceeds. To call God *Father* and deny that He begets is as absurd as to call Him a sun and deny that He enlightens. Those who believe in *peccability* choose inferiority of nature rather than inferiority of relation; thus, they become religionists who are without an Impeccable Saviour.

THE SON DECLARES THE FATHER

Jesus Christ claims the incommunicable name—I AM (Ex. 3:14; John 8:58). The name signifies unchangeable essence and ever-lasting duration. Change is written on everything earthly; Christ is unchangeable (Heb. 13:8), for He is God. The statement, "Before Abraham was, I am" (John 8:58), has no reference to Christ's coming into existence before Abraham. He never came into being. The Jews understood this to be a claim to Deity, and they took up stones to stone the Chief Corner Stone (Eph. 2:20; John 8:59) for blasphemy. They knew that the title I AM referred to Deity, but they were blinded by their religious traditions to the fact of Christ's Deity. Paul said, "But if our gospel be hid, it is hid to them that are lost: In whom the god of this world hath blinded the minds of them which believe not, lest the light of the glorious gospel of Christ, who is the image of God, should shine unto them" (II Cor. 4:3,4). The unsaved do not know Christ as God, but the saved do. Our Saviour claims pre-existence; He unveils the fact of Eternal Being, for there is no mention of His beginning or ending. *Theos,* the Greek word for God, is used in reference to Father (John 6:27), Son (Heb. 1:8), and Holy Spirit (Acts 5:3).

The gospel of John has been called the *bosom of Christ* because it reveals the heart of Christ. Christ came *from* the heart of God *to* the heart of man. He said, "I came forth from the Father, and am come into the world: again, I leave the world, and go to the Father" (John 16:28). As God said to Israel, "Ye have seen what I did unto the Egyptians, and how I bare you on eagles' wings, and brought you unto myself" (Ex. 19.4), so John portrays Christ bearing the elect of God upon the wings of sovereign grace into the presence of the Father Himself. "Father, I will that they also, whom thou has given me, be with me where I am; that they may behold my glory . . ." (John 17:24). John 16:28 gives a perfect outline to the entire gospel of John. The apostle pictures Jesus Christ: (1) Coming from the Father for His *incarnation* (1:1-18); (2) Coming into the world for our *salvation* (1:19-11:57); (3) Leaving the world for our *sanctification* (12-17); and (4) Going to the Father for our *glorification* (18-21). The first three gospels are a *presentation* of Jesus Christ; the gospel of John is an *interpretation*—it proves that Christ is the Eternal Son of God.

The aim of the incarnation was to reveal the Father. "No man hath seen God at any time; the only begotten Son, which is in the bosom of the Father, he hath declared him." God had spoken by the prophets in a piece-meal manner. He had a *Word* to spell; the Word was His own *Name*. Christ, coming from the Father, spelled the Name out in such absolute perfection as to need no one else to speak. "God, who at sundry times and in divers manners spake in time past unto the fathers by the prophets, hath in these last days spoken unto us by his Son . . ." (Heb. 1:1,2). He has spoken *once* and *twice* (Ps. 62:11) ; a *third* time He will not speak. We must not look for any additional revelation since there is nothing more to seek in the perfect revelation of Truth. Christ is the substance of the types and shadows of the Old Testament. He leaves nothing before the heart of the worshiper but His own glorious Person, Truth Incarnate.

Jesus Christ is the Eternal Logos. He was not from the beginning; He already was in the beginning. He was not only with God; He was God. No exegetical jugglery can hide the force of the truth contained in John 1:1. As a word may be distinguished from the thought it expresses (for the two are not identical), so can the Second Person of the Godhead be distinguished from the First. There cannot be a word apart from the thought behind it; neither an apprehension of the existence of "God" and the "Word" without one another. They are distinguishable but inseparable.

The Son of God has the *same substance* as the Father—"I and my Father are one" (John 10:30). Christ did not hesitate to place Himself first. He was not speaking as a subordinate, but an equal. The word *One* is not a reference to a single unit in the exact mathematical sense, but one in the sense of a compound unit—a unity which involves plurality. See (Gen. 2:24; 11:6; 41:1,5,25; I Kings 22:13; Neh. 8:1; John 17:22; Acts 4:32; I Cor. 3:8; Eph. 2:14; and I John 5:7). Two people (husband and wife) constitute one flesh; Paul the planter and Apollos the waterer are one; Jews and Gentiles are one in Christ; believers are described as being of one heart and one soul. When Christ said, "My Father," He spoke from the standpoint of His absolute Deity. Thus, ". . . my Father is greater than I" (John 14:28) contemplates Christ as Mediator —the position of subjection to the will of the Father. *There is priority of position but never inferiority of nature.* The statement, "I and my Father," affirms the unity of nature or essence—*one in every Divine perfection.* There is not one perfection to be found in the First Person of the Godhead that does not exist in the Second. This annihilates the concept of peccability. "All things that the Father hath are mine: therefore said I, that he shall take of mine, and shall shew it unto you" (John 16:15).

Jesus Christ is as eternal as the Father. He is the brightness of God's glory (Heb. 1:3). The brightness issuing from the sun is of the same nature as the sun. Brightness cannot be separated from the sun, nor can Christ be separated from the Father. The brightness, though from the sun, is not the sun itself; Jesus Christ, though from the Father, is not the Father. "Jesus said unto them, if God were your Father, ye would love me: for I proceeded forth and came from God; neither came I of myself, but he sent me" (John 8:42). As the glory of the sun is the brightness, so the glory of the Father is Christ. "And now, O Father, glorify thou me with thine own self with the glory which I had with thee before the world was" (John 17:5). "For God, who commanded the light to shine out of darkness, hath shined in our hearts, to give the light of the knowledge of the glory of God in the face of Jesus Christ" (II Cor. 4:6). As the light which the sun gives the world is by this brightness, so the light which the Father gives the world is by Christ. Christ said, "... He that hath seen me hath seen the Father ... " (John 14:9). Jesus Christ, therefore, is the brightness of God's glory; He is greater than all the sparks and flickering candles (the prophets) that preceded His incarnation. The Saviour is such brightness that He is incapable of eclipsing the Father's glory.

The Son of God is equal with the Father. Christ is the *very impress of God's substance.* "For in him (Christ) dwelleth all the fulness of the Godhead bodily" (Col. 2:9). The Greek word for *express image* means exact expression. All that God is, in His nature and character, is expressed absolutely and perfectly by the incarnate Son. As to the Son's *firm impressions of the Father's character,* He is greater than all the vanishing shadows under the law.

18

Was not Adam made in the *image* of God? If Adam, who was a peccable person, was made in the image of God; then, what about Christ being the image of God? How can an image of something be the thing of which it is the figure? The answer is not difficult to the Christian. Adam was a type of Christ, as incarnate, Who only is the express image of His Father's Person and the likeness of His excellent glory. The things in Adam were of a *created substance,* but those in Christ were *uncreated.*

The Son of God is the image of the Father's glory as the incarnate Son. His Godhead was not an image. His works were infinitely perfect by virtue of His Godhead, and this Divine perfection was revealed in the flesh. When an image is looked upon, another is seen. Thus, the Person and work of Christ manifest the perfection and glory of the Father. Philip asked Christ to manifest the Father, and the Lord Jesus replied, ". . . he that hath seen me hath seen the Father, and how sayest thou then, Shew us the Father" (John 14:9). The Father, therefore, must be seen by us through the Son in Whom all the fulness of the Godhead dwells (Col. 2:9).

How can Christ be the image of the invisible Godhead? The Deity of Christ is as invisible as the Father; but being clothed with flesh, God's works can be seen. Christ presents the excellency of the Father in figure.

Indwelling is not identity. "Believest thou not that I am in the Father, and the Father in me? the words that I speak unto you I speak not of myself; but the Father that dwelleth in me, he doeth the works" (John 14:10). A demon may dwell within a man (Luke 11:26), but that does not make the demon the man nor the man the demon. Jesus Christ is in the believer (John 15:4; Gal. 2:20; Eph. 3:17; Col. 1:27; Rev. 3:20), but that does not make Christ the believer. We are in Christ (Eph. 1.6) ; however, that does not make believers christs. As the Father must be distinct from the Son Who is in Him, so the Son must be distinct from the Father in Whom He is. The Father and Son, though of one and the same nature, cannot be one and the same Person. The doctrine Christ preached was not of Himself as man, but of the Father Who dwelt in Him.

Man could never know the Father apart from Jesus Christ. Abel, Noah, Abraham, and all the Old Testament saints knew God, but they did not know Him as Father. Here is where we need to distinguish names and titles: (1) The *name of Patriarch is Almighty;* (2) The *covenant name is Jehovah;* and (3) The *relationship name is Father.* The relationship name of Father is a revelation by Jesus Christ. Observe the number of times the word *Father* is found in John 14.

Jesus Christ came into the world not only to reveal the Father but to *redeem* the sinner. He came not, as the president of our country would go into a disaster area, to look upon the poor helpless victims; but to redeem the victims of depravity whom the Father gave Him in the covenant of redemption. Christ came not to redeem by appointed methods, but by Himself. He came not to stand by and prescribe, but to minister and provide the means of salvation. The Saviour came not only to provide salvation, but to be that salvation (I Pet. 1:18,19; Rev. 1:5).

After the Saviour finished the work of redemption, He ascended to the Father to represent the saints in their *sanctification.* Believers, having been positionally set apart by regeneration, stand in need of experimental sanctification. Sanctification is not something Jesus Christ gives believers, it is Himself in Christians. "But of him are ye in Christ Jesus, who of God is made unto us wisdom, and righteousness, and sanctification, and redemption" (I Cor. 1:30). God's method is for His men to ". . . go, stand and speak in the temple to the people *all the words of this life"* (Acts 5:20). When "all the words of this life" are preached, they will include salvation, holiness, and all the other truths related to life. This is the reason Paul said, "For I determined not to know anything among you, save Jesus Christ, and him crucified" (I Cor. 2:2).

The Saviour returned to the Father for the believer's *glorification.* Christ said, "Father, I will that they also, whom thou hast given me, be with me where I am; that they may behold my glory, which thou hast given me: for thou lovedst me before the foundation of the world" (John 17:24). Christians have been *called* unto eternal glory (I Pet. 5:10; I Thess. 2:12) ; they are *prepared* for eternal glory (Rom. 9:23; II Cor. 3:18; II Cor. 4:16,17) ; and they shall be *brought unto* eternal glory (Heb. 2:10). Our destiny therefore is glory. Glory is generally understood to be fame, fortune, and pleasure—things extraordinary and rare. All this, however, is but a dim shadow of what God means by glory; yet, out of the shadow, we may obtain a little inkling of what the substance must be. "When he (Christ) shall come to be glorified in his saints, and to be admired in all them that believe (because our testimony among you was believed) in that day" (II Thess. 1:10). Christians have an incomprehensible fortune; they are heirs of God and joint-heirs with Christ (Rom. 8:17). Only Christians know true pleasure; their pleasure is God's pleasure, for God works in them "both to will and to do of his good pleasure" (Phil. 2:13). The Psalmist said "Thou wilt shew me the path of life: in thy presence is fulness of joy; at thy right hand there are pleasures for evermore" (Ps. 16:11).

THE MYSTERY OF GODLINESS

The manifestation of God in the flesh is both a mystery and a revelation. "And without controversy great is the mystery of godliness: God was manifest in the flesh . . ." (I Tim. 3:16). Many things are made known to the understanding of natural man, but some things are impenetrable to him in his natural condition. The things of God revealed in creation are not considered mysterious. "For the invisible things of him from the creation of the world are clearly seen, being understood by the things that are made, even his eternal power and Godhead; so that they are without excuse" (Rom. 1:20). But God's manifestation of Himself is hidden from the natural man. The *manifestation of godliness* is not something about God, but God Himself. I Timothy 3:16 speaks not only of a *mystery*, but *a manifestation*. We must not become so occupied with the "mystery of godliness" that we overlook its manifestation. In order for the eternal Son to fulfill the blessed mission on which He was to embark, a body was prepared for Him (Heb. 10:5); in that body He made His appearance on earth. "(For the life was *manifested*, and we have seen it, and bear witness, and shew unto you that eternal life, which was with the Father, and was *manifested unto us*)" (I John 1:2).

The natural man has no faculty by which he can comprehend or evaluate the things of the Spirit. A great amount of controversy has emerged from the meaning of the word *natural*. Natural is used in the New Testament as indicative of an unrenewed nature. Paul said, "But the natural man receiveth not the things of the Spirit of God: for they are foolishness unto him: neither can he know them, because they are spiritually discerned" (I Cor. 2:14). The natural man is earthly, sensual, devilish, and has not the Spirit (James 3:15; Jude 19). Paul said, ". . . Now if any man have not the Spirit of Christ, he is none of his" (Rom. 8:9). Man by natural birth is so far from God that regeneration is a necessity if he is to understand the things of the Spirit. Regeneration is the communication of the principle of life to man by the operation of the Spirit. It is the work of God alone, and as far beyond the natural ability of man to perform as his first birth.

The first sin of humanity put the mind out of balance for the perception of spiritual truth. Adam became wise with a wisdom alienated from God when he partook of the forbidden fruit. Since then, man has sought to know God by processes of reason; but he has found his search to be futile. The wisdom of this world is vain—whether it be its philosophy, science, poetry, art, or religion. "For the wisdom of this world is foolishness with God . . ." (I Cor. 3:19).

When the "mystery of godliness" is driven to the heart by the Spirit, the disposition of the recipient is affected. A person knows no more of Christ than he values in Him, so his life will be brought into conformity only to the things he esteems. When the things which he claims to respect do not work practical godliness in his life, he has but *a human knowledge of Divine things.* Christianity is not a mere mental assent to certain Biblical truths, but godliness which follows holiness (Heb. 12:14).

Godliness is either the principle of Christianity, or the inward disposition of the soul toward God. The inherent cause of godliness is Jesus Christ. The faith of God's elect acknowledges the truth which is after godliness (Titus 1:1). But the non-elect ". . . consent not to wholesome words, even the words of our Lord Jesus Christ, and to the doctrine which is according to godliness; He is proud, knowing nothing, but doting about questions and strifes of words, whereof cometh envy, strife, railings, evil surmisings, perverse disputings of men of corrupt minds, and destitute of the truth, supposing that gain is godliness: from such withdraw thyself" (I Tim. 6:3-5).

The mysteries of God should not cause man to despair. The excellency of the Teacher Who is the Holy Spirit, not the natural ability of the scholar, unveils these things to the heart of man. The Holy Spirit gives discernment where He finds none. He has a prerogative over all other teachers; He not only teaches the mysteries of God, but gives enlightenment and understanding. Christ said, "All things that the Father hath are mine: therefore said I, that he shall take of mine, and shall shew it unto you" (John 16:15). The Saviour was talking to His disciples about the prerogative of the Holy Spirit. John said, "But the anointing which ye have received of him abideth in you, and ye need not that any man teach you: but as the same anointing teacheth you of all things, and is truth, and is no lie, and even as it hath taught you, ye shall abide in him" (I John 2:27).

Godliness is not only a mystery, but a *great* mystery. Paul does not call godliness riches, but *unsearchable riches* (Eph. 3:8). When he speaks of its fruit, he says it *passes knowledge* (Eph. 3:19). It is great because of the Persons involved in it. God the Father, Son, and Holy Spirit had a part in the "mystery of godliness." So great is this mystery that the angels desired to look into it (I Pet. 1:12). The greatness is consummated by bringing God and man together. God, Who descended from the height of heaven to God manifest in the flesh, brings man from the depth of sin to the height of grace.

To be and *to be manifested* are two different things. God has always been in existence, but He has not always been manifested. In order to manifest Himself He had to be abased. Man's natural desire is to hide his abasement. If things go well with him, he wants the trumpet blown and the alarm sounded; however, if things go ill, he says, "Tell it not in Gath, publish it not in the streets . . ." (II Sam. 1:20). The Pharisee publicizes his success, but he will go to any extent to hide his failure. But Jesus Christ abhorred not to become flesh; He despised not to have His condescension manifestly known. His poor manger was manifested by a star (Matt. 2:2, 11); His destitute earthly existence was visible by the fact that He had no place to lay His head; His shameful death was published by a great eclipse; finally, the abasement of Christ is to be displayed to the whole world by the proclamation of the gospel. Paul said, "O foolish Galatians, who hath bewitched you, that ye should not obey the truth, before whose eyes Jesus Christ hath been *evidently set forth*, crucified among you?" (Gal. 3:1). We are concerned with both mystery and manifestation.

The "mystery of godliness," though it is *now* revealed, *is still a mystery*. It remains a mystery because we cannot, by searching into the depths of it, fully comprehend it. The "mystery of godliness" was concealed from all men until God brought it forth from His own bosom. God, Who decreed that man would fall, devised a plan to save fallen man by the death of His Son. Salvation by the death of Christ was a plan devised by the Trinity; it was hidden in the secret closet of God's bosom. This great mystery was brought forth from the bosom of the Father when the *Word was made flesh* and tabernacled among men. This mystery is now revealed, but it is manifested to only the chosen. "So the last shall be first, and the first last: for many be called, but *few chosen*" (Matt. 20:16). It was revealed to the elect Jews of the Old Testament by being wrapped in ceremonies and types, but it was hidden from the rest of mankind under the covering of the same ceremonies and types. When Jesus Christ came, He was revealed to the elect Jews and Gentiles; but the rest of mankind were blinded. Paul said, "Even so then at this present time there is *a remnant according to the election of grace.* And if by grace, then it is no more of works: otherwise grace is no more grace. But if it be of works, then it is no more grace: otherwise work is no more work. What then? Israel hath not obtained that which he seeketh for; *but the election hath obtained it,* and the rest were blinded" (Rom. 11:5-7).

Godliness is a mystery to the elect. Although they see some part of it, they do not see it fully. It is a mystery in regard to what they do not know. They see Divine things wrapped in the mirror of the *written Word,* but there will be a clearer sight when they see the face of God in Christ. The sight which the elect have now is small in comparison with what they shall have in heaven (I John 3:2, 3). Is there not an element of mystery in all the graces? For example, there is peace in turmoil, rest in bondage, strength in weakness, and gain in loss. There is a glorious assembly hidden under the scorn of the world. The Church is in the world, but she is not of the world. She has life, but it is a hidden (mystical) life (Col. 3:1-4). Christians, therefore, are a strange kind of people—poor, yet rich; living, yet dying; glorious, yet base (II Cor. 8:9; 4:10-12; I Cor. 1:2; 4:9, 10).

The true Church (the elect of God) is a company of people for whom God cares more than all the rest of mankind. The world stands for the sake of the Church, and not the Church for the world—except to gather all the members of the elect family (Acts 15:14; II Pet. 3:9). Christ is the Head of His Body which is the Church; therefore, it is natural for the Body to be conformed to the Head. Since the Son of God wrought our salvation in a state of abasement, Christians should work out this salvation in humility (Phil. 2:12). God sanctifies afflictions and poverty for the spiritual good of His people. Pride feeds upon some *outward* or *inward* excellency. To take away Paul's *inward* excellence, God gave him a thorn in the flesh; to remove his *outward* excellence, God gave the apostle persecution and poverty (II Cor. 11:16-28; 12:1-7). Shall we complain against God's providence if it goes contrary to *our* desires? Is not God's desire for us greater than our own? His care for us is seen in His providence. The glory of God, in the Church, is brighter when the Church is outwardly abased. It was more evident in the days of the Church's persecution than it is in the day of religious prosperity.

The greatness of the mystery is Jesus Christ. Therefore, the "mystery of godliness" is godliness (piety characterized by a God-ward attitude) embodied in and communicated through the doctrine of Jesus Christ (II John 9-11). This greatness is without controversy because it is confessedly great. The word *controversy* in the Greek is also translated *confessedly.* "And confessedly great is the mystery of piety: Who was manifested in the flesh." The Divine Name does not appear in the oldest manuscripts, but that does not destroy the greatness of the subject. *Who* was made flesh and dwelt among men? The Word, the eternal *Logos,* was made flesh. The eternal *Logos* was ". . . justified in the Spirit, seen of angels, preached unto the Gentiles, believed on in the world, received up into glory." So great is this "mystery of godliness," that it makes the persons associated with it *great.* What made John the Baptist greater than all the prophets and others who preceded him? He saw Christ come in the flesh. "Verily I say unto you, Among them that are born of women there hath not risen a greater than John the Baptist . . ." (Matt. 11:11). The comparison is between degrees of light and opportunity, not their persons. What made those after John greater than he? They saw Christ ascend to glory after He had finished the work of redemption. John was not blessed by this wonderful sight. ". . . Notwithstanding he that is least in the kingdom of heaven is greater than he" (Matt. 11:11). Consider the Christian's present sight of Jesus Christ—dead, buried, raised, glorified, and seated at the Father's right hand!

Persons know no more of Jesus Christ than they value and esteem in Him. With this fact before us, what do those who believe in peccability value and esteem in Christ? The teachers of peccability make, in their desire to produce a gospel relevant to modern man, the tragic mistake of losing their relevance to God, Christ, and the salvation of depraved men. Their evaluation of the Son of God is so low that they see in Him no more than they see in any religious leader. Such serious departure from the high esteem of Impeccability is a *damnable heresy,* and the warning about it is as relevant

26

now as it was when Peter gave his warning: "But there were *false prophets* also among the people . . . , who privily shall bring in *damnable heresies,* even denying the Lord that bought them, and bring upon themselves swift destruction" (II Pet. 2:1).

THE MANIFESTATION OF GODLINESS

There are three Persons in the Godhead, but only one of the Persons is manifested. "And without controversy great is the mystery of godliness: God was manifest in the flesh" (I Tim. 3:16). The manifestations of God's *character* and *perfection* are revealed in the world, Church, providence, and the written Word. These are manifestations of character and perfection; whereas, *"The manifestation of godliness"* is the manifestation of God Himself. There is a manifestation of the Father in His children; a manifestation of the Son in those whom He is not ashamed to call His brethren, and a manifestation of the Spirit in all whom He regenerates. These are manifestations of Persons although they are not personal manifestations of the Godhead. I Timothy 3:16 speaks of a personal manifestation of God—God in the second Person was manifested. The Father, Son, and Holy Spirit are all God, but they were not all *made flesh.*

We are told that the Holy Spirit came down in bodily form like a dove, but the Holy Spirit was not a dove. The dove was only a symbol of the Holy Spirit in purity, peace, sensitivity, and discernment. The eternal Son of God was manifested in the incarnation as Son of Man. God was manifest in the flesh by clothing Himself in human nature. He assumed the nature into His Person so that God the Son and the Man Christ Jesus were not two Persons, but one Person with two natures.

The union of the Divine and human natures is not like any other union. It is unlike that union between soul and body of man; body and soul compose but one nature between them. Christ's union with believers cannot be compared with the union of the Divine and human natures in Christ, for the distinct personality of both Christ and believers is maintained. Nor is it like the union among the Persons of the Trinity. In Christ there is One Person and two natures; in the Trinity there are three Persons and one nature.

Why was God revealed in the Son? Only the One Who possesses the "image of God" (Heb. 1:3) can restore fallen man to his rightful *image.* The word "image" involves the two ideas of *representation and manifestation.* Man was created in God's image, and after His likeness; therefore, man was created as a visible manifestation of God for the purpose of representing God on the earth. Though man was created for this purpose, his fall prevented him from being a perfect vehicle for the representation of God. Christ, Who is the perfect "image of God," *renews* the elect ". . . in knowledge after the image of him that created him" (Col. 3:10).

Jesus Christ has *power over all flesh*. "As thou hast given him power over all flesh, that he should give eternal life to as many as thou hast given him" (John 17:2). Power over all flesh denotes authority over all creatures. Unless Christ has power over all flesh, there could be no salvation of the lost. Every obstacle must be removed from the sinner for the entrance of the light of God's glory to the heart. Earth and hell are united to oppose those whom the Father has given the Son, but Christ is given power over all opposition. It is not enough that hindrances be removed; one must be qualified to enjoy eternal life. He Who gives eternal life as Mediator supplies the qualification for the enjoyment of it. To bestow eternal life on lost sinners is the glory of the Father; to be the means and channel for the application of that eternal life is the glory of the Son—Who was made flesh.

God absolutely considered cannot be seen. "No man hath seen God at any time; the only begotten Son, which is in the bosom of the Father, he hath declared him" (John 1:18). When one thinks of God absolutely, without thinking of Him as manifested in the flesh, he considers Him only in the capacity of the invisible God. "Who only hath immortality, dwelling in the light which no man can approach unto; whom no man hath seen, nor can see: to whom be honour and power everlasting. Amen" (I Tim. 6:16). "God manifest in the flesh," however, can be seen; this was made possible by the incarnation. "(For the life was manifested, and we have seen it, and bear witness, and shew unto you that eternal life, which was with the Father, and was manifested unto us)" (I John 1:2). God absolutely considered cannot be approached, but God manifest in the flesh can be; therefore, we have access to the Father through Jesus Christ (Eph. 2:18; Heb. 4:14-16). "Having therefore, brethren, boldness to enter into the holiest by the blood of Jesus, By a new and living way, which he hath consecrated for us, through the veil, that is to say, his flesh; And having an high priest over the house of God; Let us draw near with a true heart in full assurance of faith, having our hearts sprinkled from an evil conscience, and our bodies washed with pure water" (Heb. 10:19-22). Thinking of God absolutely devours one's thoughts, but to think of God manifest in the flesh is a comforting consideration. For example, to see the sun alone in its glory and lustre is impossible without blinding the eye; but to see the sun in eclipse, shaded by the shadow of the earth, is possible to the naked eye. No man can see God absolutely, but *to see God in the flesh is to see Him in eclipse.*

God absolutely considered is a consuming fire Who demands justice and condemnation, but "God manifest in the flesh" is a purifying fire Who gives satisfaction and grace with commendation. Every person is related to God either as a "consuming fire" *without blood,* or as a "consuming fire" *with* blood. Fire *without* blood is *condemnation;* fire *with* blood is *commendation.* The children of Israel were blessed in the offerings they made because the offerings included both "fire" and "blood" (Lev. 1-5). The "live coal" that was taken from off the altar purified Isaiah's lips (Is. 6:5-8) because it came from off the altar where the offering of blood was made by fire. If the "live coal" had not come from the altar of sacrifice, Isaiah would have been destroyed. The sacrifice of blood gave the fire a purifying rather than a destroying effect. On the contrary, it will be well to observe the results of *fire and no blood.* Sodom and Gomorrah and Nadab and Abihu were destroyed by fire because there was no sacrifice of blood. Men will suffer the eternal fire of hell because they reject the blood of Jesus Christ. "... without the shedding of blood is no remission" (Heb. 9:22).

The Lord Jesus took not upon Himself the nature of angels; He veiled Himself "in the likeness of sinful flesh." "For what the law could not do, in that it was weak through the flesh, God sending his own Son in the likeness of sinful flesh, and for sin condemned sin in the flesh" (Rom. 8:3). Professing Christendom is taught that Christ is like unto themselves. Christ is unlike man, however, because in this "likeness" He lifts the elect from the pit of depravity into the likeness of Himself. Jesus Christ was sent, *not in the likeness of flesh,* but in flesh. He was sent, however, *not in sinful flesh,* but in the likeness of sinful flesh. Nothing can more clearly prove that the Lord Jesus Christ, though He assumed human nature, took it without taint of sin or corruption. Christ was not made in the likeness of the flesh of unfallen man, but in the likeness of man's fallen flesh. There was no corruption in Christ's human nature, but He had all the *sinless infirmities* of that nature. The word *"likeness" refers not to the word "flesh," but to the word "sinful."* Thus, the Lord Jesus took unto Himself our nature—*sin excepted*—in order that He might take us unto Himself—after sin was put away by the sacrifice of Himself.

Christ is manifested in the mortal flesh of Christians. "Always bearing about in the body the dying of the Lord Jesus, that the life also of Jesus might be made manifest in our body. For we which live are alway delivered unto death for Jesus' sake, that the life also of Jesus might be made manifest in our mortal flesh" (II Cor. 4:10, 11). As the flesh of Christ was first set apart, then abased, and then glorified; so the flesh of every Christian must be content to be first set apart, then abased in service for Christ, and then glorified. This is the Divine order, and there is no short cut from sanctification to glorification.

Christians must ever take heed of pride. The Son of God emptied Himself; shall His children be full of pride? Christ made Himself of no reputation; shall His sheep stand upon their honor? The Lord Jesus Christ took upon Himself the form of a servant; shall His people be lords to be ministered to and not to minister? Some believers may feel too proud to imitate humble men, but they must not think themselves too good to follow the humble Saviour. Christ must be manifest in our flesh; consequently, when a person sees a Christian, he sees Christ manifest in him.

Have Christians forgotten, in this age of religious tolerance, how the Saviour lived and died? The saints do not bear the dying of the Lord Jesus "in the body" by wearing a cross on their persons, nor by sitting on the pinnacle of religious praise and honor. To bear "in the body" the dying of the Lord Jesus is to bear the stigma of the cross for the sake of the gospel. *What is the gospel? It is the truth of the Person and Work of the Impeccable Saviour.* Bearing in the body the dying of the Lord Jesus is not something borne occasionally—when it is convenient or expedient—but always. The Christian who always uncompromisingly stands up for the Impeccable Saviour knows what it is to always bear "in his body" the "dying of the Lord Jesus."

Nadab and Abihu were destroyed by God's consuming fire because they offered "strange fire" before the Lord (Lev. 10: 1, 2). The "strange fire" was a foreign substance introduced to the Divine system. There is only one way to obey God, and that is by doing what He commands. There are always some who try to materialize the supernatural. This is what Nadab and Abihu did. "Strange fire" is but a human imitation of that which is Divine. To be preserved from what is "strange," there must be the confession of "Jesus Christ come in flesh" (I John 4:1-3). In what kind of flesh did the Son of God make His appearance? Was His flesh peccable or Impeccable? If it was peccable, then He was disqualified as saviour; but if it was Impeccable, then He was qualified as the Saviour. Those who teach peccability are offering "strange fire"; they shall, like Nadab and Abihu, be destroyed for their introduction of a foreign message into the Divine system.

THE INCARNATION

The *faith of the gospel* has had to be defended in every generation —ours is no different. Many are now saying that the incarnation of the eternal Son is positive mythology. The "New Theology" teaches that humanity is divine in essence, and Christ came to the consciousness of the identity with God. They say the incarnation is in mankind; God realizes himself in his universe, supremely in man and typically in Jesus Christ. They accuse orthodoxy of restricting the description, "God manifest in the flesh," to Jesus Christ alone; they would extend it in a lesser degree to all humanity. The incarnation is, according to this heretical concept, not God condescending to become man, but man ascending to be god. This heresy carries us no further than man himself, but the Truth of the Gospel carries believing sinners into the arms of the infinite God.

Christ's *Incarnation* is the foundation truth upon which Christianity rests. "And the Word was made flesh, and dwelt among us . . ." (John 1:14). Jesus Christ is not God *mutilated* by the flesh, but God *manifest* in the flesh (I Tim. 3:16). The Person of Christ was not deprived of absolute perfection by His manifestation in the flesh, nor did He surrender His oneness with the Father. Our Lord used the word *flesh* (John 1:14; I Tim. 3:16) to signify nature, for *flesh* is not a person. Had He used the term *man*, He would have meant a *person;* thus, He would have made Himself two persons rather than *One Person with two natures*. Jesus Christ is not *a man*, but *the Son of Man* (John 3:13). So important is the incarnation that the Bible says, " . . . Every spirit that *confesseth* that Jesus Christ is come in the flesh is of God: And every spirit that *confesseth not* that Jesus Christ is come in the flesh is not of God: and this is the spirit of antichrist . . ." (I John 4:2,3). The denial of the incarnation is two-fold: "not of God" is *negative,* and "of antichrist" is *positive*. Denial of the absolute perfection of Christ's Person (His Impeccability) can be attributed only to the spirit of antichrist.

There is an *inward test* to which every person is subjected with regard to the incarnation. " . . . And hereby we know that he abideth in us, by the Spirit which he hath given us" (I John 3:24). The *subjective Spirit* confesses the *objective fact* that "Jesus Christ is come in the flesh." The reason for such confession, on the part of the Spirit, is that He had so much to do with the flesh in which Christ came. He prepared for Him an Impeccable body—that Holy of Holies—wherein the "Godhead dwelleth bodily" (Col. 2:9). It is the *flesh* of Christ that brings Him within the range of the Spirit's gracious care. He said, "The Spirit of the Lord is upon me, because he hath anointed me to preach the gospel to the poor . . ." (Luke 4:18). ". . . for God giveth not the Spirit by measure unto him" (John 3:34). Christ's human nature was animated and sustained by the Spirit. He was not only *made* and *lived* in the flesh, but also *suffered* in the flesh (I Pet. 3:18). He gave His flesh to be the life of the world (John 6:51; Heb. 10: 19-22). As the purpose of the Holy Spirit is to animate and sustain the flesh of Christ, so also it is His object to make the elect of God one with Christ Who is come in the flesh. To deny that "Jesus Christ is come in the flesh" is to deny the Father. "Whosoever denieth the Son, the same hath not the Father . . ." (I John 2:23). Faith, which is the gift of God, knows that the human nature of Christ is as Impeccable as His Divine nature.

The work of the *Godhead* is included in the "Word made flesh." There are many religionists who deny the Trinity; but if there is no Trinity, there is no incarnation; hence, no objective redemption. If there is no objective Redeemer, then man is without a Mediator. Redemption was not purchased by the Father Who *planned* it, nor by the Holy Spirit Who *applies* it. Our salvation was purchased by the Eternal Son Who offered Himself through the Eternal Spirit. Consequently, He accomplished eternal redemption for the elect. (See Eph. 1:3-14; John 3:16; Heb. 9:14.)

There are three great dispensations corresponding to, and successively manifesting, the three Persons of the Godhead in the history of redemption. The dispensation of the Father began with creation and continued to the beginning of Christ's public ministry. The dispensation of the Son was the important period in which redemption was worked out objectively. It began with Christ's public ministry and continued to the day of Pentecost. That of the Holy Spirit began with His descent on the day of Pentecost and continues to the end of the age. It is the work of the Holy Spirit to *subjectively* apply the redemption which was *objectively* purchased by Jesus Christ on the cross and *electively* purposed by the Father (John 3:8; II Thess. 2:13; I Pet. 1:22).

Jesus Christ did not cease to be God in the incarnation; He only veiled His Deity "in the likeness of sinful flesh" (Rom. 8:3). He did not take upon Himself all that we are in Adam, but took *part* of the same (Heb. 2:14). "Wherefore in all things it behoved him to be *made like unto his brethren* . . ." (Heb. 2:17). Christ did not identify Himself with the *fallen* race, but *with man viewed in Divine grace*. The statement, "his brethren," refers to their election in eternity; this is according to the eternal purpose of God (Eph. 3:11). His incarnation, which was in *time* (Gal. 4:4; II Tim. 1:9, 10), was not only for those brethren who preceded—in time—His incarnation; but for all those who shall believe on Him—in time to come—through the word of the apostles (John 17:20). It was proper that He should be like them in nature—as viewed in Divine grace—and thus be *free from any contamination of the fallen Adamic nature*. He calls them "His brethren." " . . . He that sanctifieth and they who are sanctified are all of one . . . " (Heb. 2:11).

The mysterious part of the incarnation was not publicly proclaimed until after Christ's resurrection. There is not a single allusion to the Divine production of Christ's human nature throughout His earthly ministry. He often called Himself the Son of God and spoke of God as His Father, but He never mentioned the miraculous conception of His human nature in the womb of Mary. None of the companions of Christ doubted that He was a man; they were convinced that there was something extraordinary about Him. ". . . What manner of man is this, that even the wind and the sea obey him" (Mark 4:41).

The fact that Christ was publicly known as "Jesus of Nazareth, the son of Joseph" (John 1:45) is irrelevant to the question of His virgin birth. (See Matt. 13:55; Luke 2:27,33,48; Mark 6:3.) Both Matthew and Luke show how the expressions "son of Joseph," "the parents," and "thy father and I" are to be understood. Joseph and Mary were *espoused* (an ancient custom as binding as wedlock itself) by a *special providence* to protect Mary from being accused of harlotry. The Bible says ". . . before they came together, she was found with child of the Holy Ghost" (Matt. 1:18). The conception and birth of Christ cannot be determined by the laws of evidence in the same way as the resurrection. There were eyewitnesses to the resurrection; there were none, apart from God, to the miraculous conception. God had done something new that would never be repeated in the earth; therefore, there was no analogy by which to explain it. If no mother knows the manner of her natural conception, what presumption to question the manner in which the Son of God took flesh of the man whom He created! Was it not as easy for God to make the body of the Second Adam in the womb of Mary as to make the body of the first Adam out of the dust of the earth?

The Lord Jesus hid *the glory of His eternal nativity under the veil of an earthly nativity*. This subject deserves our most serious consideration. The glories of Christ are threefold: *personal* (essential), which is His from all eternity; *official,* the glory given Him in the offices to which He had been set apart; and *moral,* the glory which had been given Him and could be given the disciples (John 17:22). Christ's essential glory was veiled by flesh, except where faith apprehended it. His official glory was also veiled; He did not walk through the earth in His official capacity, for He was a Servant. But His moral glory could not be hid; *He could not be less than perfect in everything* since He was the Impeccable Savior. His perfect life qualified Him to be the "one perfect sacrifice for sin" (Heb. 10:10,14). Since He was *free from sin,* He was the efficient *sacrifice for sin.*

The union of two natures in one Person (the God-Man) is the great mystery of Godliness. Paul gives the *norm* for Christology (Phil. 2:5-11). The "form of God" declares His Deity; the "form of a servant" asserts His humanity. Though there was no inequality in His essential Being, He did not selfishly choose to remain in the enjoyment of that blessed condition. Therefore, He emptied Himself, taking the "form of a servant" and becoming obedient unto death. He did not consider His condescension *robbery* when He veiled His essential glory during the days of His earthly sojourn. The contrast is between His existence in the "form of God" and in the "form of a servant." It seems clear, from the context, that we have a *change of form—not of content.* He did not surrender His Divine nature, but He took a human nature. Thus, we have an *unfallen human nature* united to the Divine nature in one indivisible Person—the *Impeccable Christ.* This union, in theological circles, is called the *Hypostatic Union.*

The *Hypostatic Union* removes any possibility of Christ having the capacity for sin. He would have been capable of sinning only by a completely free opposition of His human will to the Divine will. That was impossible since the controlling agent of His human will was the eternal *Logos*. (See John 4:34; 5:30; 6:38; 8:29; Rom. 15:3.) Christ had a free human will, but the *I* that was active through it was God. It was not a human but a Divine Self Who was responsible for the deeds performed through the human will. If the human nature had been the basis of His personality, He would not have been the *God-Man* (I Tim. 2:5)—but the *man-God*.

You will observe, with respect to the union of the Divine and human natures of Christ, some deeds performed in one nature and ascribed to the other. For example, in His human nature He is called the Son of Man; yet, under this title He is described by an attribute which belongs to His Divine nature. Christ said, ". . . no man hath ascended up to heaven, but he that came down from heaven, even the Son of man which is in heaven" (John 3:13). Omnipresence is an attribute belonging only to the Divine nature. On the other hand, you will find Him doing things—in the Divine nature—which are ascribed to His human nature. The Scripture says, "The Lord of Glory was crucified" (I Cor. 2:8). Crucifixion cannot be attributed to the Son of God in His Divine nature. God, Who has eternal existence, cannot be crucified. His human nature did not act independently of the Divine, nor the Divine of the human; consequently, all His acts were the actions of one indivisible Person acting in the fulness of both natures. Therefore, the various names respecting the Person of Christ are used interchangeably in regard to His two natures.

THE VIRGIN BIRTH

The union of the Divine and human natures was accomplished, in the incarnation of Christ, by the power of the Spirit in the womb of the virgin Mary. "Now the birth of Jesus Christ was on this wise: When as his mother Mary was espoused to Joseph, *before they came together,* she was found with child of the Holy Ghost" (Matt. 1:18). Some argue that the word "virgin" simply means an unmarried woman. The birth of a child to a woman is no miracle. There have been many unmarried women who have, to their shame, given birth to babies; but for a virgin to give birth to a child is indeed a miracle. The time had come for the eternal purpose of God to be fulfilled—the Saviour was to be born of a virgin. The incarnation, prophesied in Genesis 3:15, was fulfilled in the "seed of the woman." A virgin bearing a Son was a *sign* (Is. 7:14) —thus a miracle. If Jesus Christ had come into the world like all other men, then He would have been no different from them in other respects. This would have disqualified Christ from being the Saviour of men.

There are some religionists who place no importance on the virgin birth. They pass by all mention of the virgin birth, miracles, and physical resurrection of Christ. They say that good Christians differ sincerely concerning these matters. Their followers are encouraged not to worry about it if they cannot believe these things. This vividly describes the theological heresy our generation faces.

The cry of the day is unity. There is a spiritual unity of which the Bible has much to say (Ps. 133:1; John 17:21). We believe in unity, but let us never forget that the unity of the body is dependent upon its life. When life departs, the body crumbles and its members are separated. How can there be any basis for unity among people when some believe in the virgin birth and some do not? The virgin birth is so basic to the incarnation that it leaves no room for compromise. *Conviction is greater than conformity.* True unity is not something that men can *make* or *promote,* but Christians are exhorted to *keep* (Eph. 4:3). The only basis for unity is the life of God which comes to the true believer through the incarnation. "Who hath saved us, and called us with an holy calling, not according to our works, but according to his own purpose and grace, which was given us in Christ Jesus before the world began, But is now made manifest by the appearing of our Saviour Jesus Christ, who hath abolished death, and hath brought life and immortality to light through the gospel" (II Tim. 1:9,10).

Christ's incarnation demanded a perfect human nature. The eternal Son has come forth: (1) From everlasting—His place with God in the beginning; (2) From Bethlehem—the place of His birth in time; and (3) From the womb of the virgin—the place of the union of the Divine and human natures in one Person—the Impeccable Saviour (Micah 5:2, Luke 1:35). *His coming through the womb of the virgin was in order that He might have a perfect human nature.* The eternal Son assumed a nature—not a person— in the incarnation. The *nature* is called the "holy thing," "seed of Abraham," and the "form of a servant" (Luke 1:35, Heb. 2:16; Phil. 2:6-8). The *Assumer* and the *assumed* cannot be the same. Nevertheless, the Assumer is perfect; the assumed must also be perfect. His Deity required the virgin birth because there is a difference between His humanity and ours. The Incorruptible could not unite with the corruptible; the Holy could not unite with the unholy.

Our Saviour's sinlessness required the virgin birth. Birth could not, of itself, secure Christ's human nature from pollution. Mary is no less a sinner than Joseph, for she said, "And my spirit hath rejoiced in God *my Saviour*" (Luke 1:47). As God protected Christ's human nature from the pollution of Joseph, so He also protected it from the pollution of Mary by the Spirit in the miraculous conception. She was elected to fulfill the essential *passive* part in the Saviour's human nature; God was the *active* Agent in the performance of the miracle.

Why do Mark and John omit any reference to the virgin birth? This is the question raised by those who object to the miracle of the incarnation. Those who take a naturalistic view of Christ's Person refuse to recognize any supernatural element in His life. If a person doubts the virgin birth because Mark does not mention it, doubt might also be cast upon the fact that Jesus Christ was born at all; he does not mention the birth. John taught that those who believed were not spiritually "born of the will of the flesh" (John 1:13); consequently, Jesus Christ was not physically born of the will of the flesh.

False teachers argue that neither Paul nor any of the apostles ever mentioned the virgin birth. They say that the apostles did not know about it, or they would have mentioned it in their writings. This would be equivalent to saying they did not believe in the existence of Mary because they never mentioned her. The fact is, Paul does speak of *"the second man from heaven"* (I Cor. 15:47), and "God sent forth his Son made of a woman" (Gal. 4:4). The apostles believed and taught the sinlessness of Jesus Christ. Is not this proof that He was without a human father? Every child of sinful Adam is a sinner by nature (Rom. 5:12) ; however, our Saviour is sinless, and this proves that His human nature is not the same as that of the sinner. It cannot be denied that the apostles believed and taught the incarnation. We do not trace the truths of the resurrection, sinlessness, and Deity of Jesus Christ *from* the virgin birth; but *to* it. If these truths be granted, surely the virgin birth becomes a necessity.

The *conception of Christ* in the womb of the virgin is beyond our comprehension. We are not to speak of the virgin birth as the immaculate conception (Luke 1:47). That is the religious dogma of some that Mary was conceived and born without original sin. Neither should it be referred to as supernatural conception because that is true of Isaac, nor miraculous birth since the birth itself was no different from others. We understand that *virgin and conception are joined without the loss of virginity,* and this was accomplish·d by the Holy Spirit. According to nature, virginity is gone before conception; but this instance is a sign (miracle) which is above nature. Natural things are based upon reason; supernatural things are based on faith. This is supernatural, and the power of the Spirit is the reason for the miracle. The angel concluded, "For with God nothing shall be impossible" (Luke 1:37). Mary asked, " ... How shall this be ... ?" (Luke 1:34) ; but she rested in the angel's resolution, " ... My soul doth magnify the Lord, And my spirit hath rejoiced in God my Saviour" (Luke 1:46,47). As Mary rested in this resolution, so must we.

To conceive is more than to receive. A vessel is not said to conceive the water that is poured into it. The reason is that it does not yield anything of itself. The virgin, however, *gave* and *took something* in the conception. She gave of her substance for the making of the body, but the Holy Spirit was the power by which the body was made. He was the *active efficient cause* in the production of the body; the virgin Mary was the *passive material cause*. The conception was a miracle and is called an overshadowing. The preposition "of" (Luke 1:35) must not be understood for the material cause but the efficient cause.

The conception of Christ took place *before Joseph and Mary came together* in legal wedlock. It is true that Matthew speaks of Joseph as a husband and Mary as a wife, but this can be accounted for under the Hebrew law of betrothal which constituted a legal contract between the parties concerned. Marriage in Israel was a covenant of two parts: the first, the betrothal period; the second, the established marriage union. The betrothal period was so binding that sexual unfaithfulness during that time was equivalent to infidelity in the established marriage relationship. The law states, "If a damsel that is a virgin be betrothed unto an husband, and a man find her in the city, and lie with her; Then ye shall bring them both out unto the gate of that city, and ye shall stone them with stones that they die ... " (Deut. 22:23,24). Matthew asserts that before this marriage was consummated she was discovered to be with child by the action of the Holy Spirit.

How did Mary go about hiding her conception? Mary the unwed, knowing she was to be a mother, ran to the fountainhead of law and judgment. She could not wait until she had imparted the good news to Elisabeth, the wife of the officiating high priest. The assurance of God's presence with her destroyed all thought of fear. The presence of Christ in the womb of Mary made John in the womb of Elisabeth leap for joy (Luke 1:41,44). How could this be apart from the sovereign power of the Spirit? There was no fear of being stoned to death for two reasons: (1) She knew that her conception was of the Holy Spirit; therefore, she was not a harlot; and (2) She had faith in the Sovereign God and knew He would fulfill His promise to give the Saviour.

The tremendous honor bestowed upon Mary must not be passed by without looking at the awful burden coupled with the honor. It is always thus in the world. Honor and reproach go hand in hand. The virgin was told, "(Yea, a sword shall pierce through thy own soul also) ... " (Luke 2:35). She knew what others did not know. Even Joseph had to wait for an answer as to her virginity. The Jews accusingly said, " ... We be not born of fornication ... " (John 8:41); they were saying they were not bastards.

Mary knew the reproach, but she also knew the honor that accompanied it. Such is the dual experience of every Christian. We no sooner experience the blessing of salvation, made possible by the Impeccable Saviour, than we find ourselves going outside the camp bearing His reproach (Heb. 13:13).

It is proper, at this point, that some consideration be given to the step-father of Jesus Christ. Joseph was Christ's legal, but not His actual, father. Had Joseph been His actual father, He would have been barred from David's throne (Jer. 22:28-30; Matt. 1:11). No descendant of Coniah (Greek—Jechonias) is to sit on the throne of David, yet the Lord Jesus is to sit on that throne (Luke 1:32). Christ born of the virgin Mary could, through the royal line in Mary's genealogy, inherit the throne. The Jewish law required genealogy through a father. This requirement was fulfilled when Joseph married Mary after the birth of Christ. Joseph was a righteous man and did not act hastily when he heard about Mary, but waited for God to give the answer (Matt. 1:19,20,24,25). If the Lord Jesus had been an illegitimate child, He could not have been a member of the congregation of Israel (Deut. 23:2) ; consequently, all His descendants would be excluded.

Jesus Christ died because He said that God was His Father (Luke 22:66-71). Caiaphas, who conducted the trial of the Saviour, could only say that the law stated that He ought to die. He was crucified, from the viewpoint of man, for just one offense—He said God was His Father. This constituted blasphemy under the Jewish law; and if His claim was not true, He deserved to die. But where was Mary during this time? Did she stand there with mouth closed to save her own reputation? The only explanation of her silence is that Jesus Christ died for a clearly stated fact—*He was the Son of God.*

The virgin birth is the manner by which the human nature of Jesus Christ is clear of original sin. Had it been otherwise, the human nature would have been infested with original sin. Deity is not humanity, nor humanity Deity; nevertheless, it must be acknowledged that He is the God-Man. This is possible because the names "Word" and "Man" refer to the Person of Jesus Christ Who possesses both natures. Thus, by virtue of this union, Jesus Christ bears the office of Mediator; *He exercises this office in both natures,* for a " . . . mediator is not a mediator *of one, but God is one*" (Gal. 3:20).

CHRIST'S HUMAN NATURE

The human nature of Christ must be distinguished from the fallen human nature of man. Our Saviour saw nothing but sin and misery from Adam to the day of Judgment. He said, "That which is born of the flesh is flesh..." (John 3:6). The word *flesh* refers to the fallen human nature. Fallen human nature has neither grace nor truth in it, but the human nature of Christ was full of grace and truth. "And the Word was made flesh, and dwelt among us (and we beheld his glory, the glory as of the only begotten of the Father,) full of grace and truth" (John 1:14). All the sons of Adam come into the world *in sinful flesh,* but Jesus Christ came *"in likeness of sinful flesh"* (Rom. 8:3). *Likeness* is not connected with *flesh,* for Christ came in real flesh. However, *likeness* is linked with *sinful* since Christ's flesh looked like the flesh of fallen man. The *"likeness of men"* (Phil. 2:7) does not lessen the reality of the human nature which Christ assumed, but it does intimate a vital difference between the flesh of Christ and that of fallen man. Christ's human nature cannot be understood apart from the right concept of *original uprightness* and *original sin.*

The most significant thing about *original uprightness* is the fact that Adam was created in God's image and after His likeness (Gen. 1:26). He was created in a state of conformity to some rule; this rule was the law of God. The law of God is the only perfect, immutable, and eternal rule. For Adam to be made upright, the rule itself was implied. How could it be said that he was made upright if there were no prescribed form by which to measure uprightness? Adam did not have, as was the case with Israel, the law written upon tables of stone; it was written upon his mind. The knowledge of uprightness was created in him. This uprightness was not essential to his being, for then he could not have lost it without the loss of his very being. Nevertheless, it was to him *as man* a natural thing; he was created with original uprightness. As a created being, he was *a dependent person.*

Unfallen Adam possessed such affections as love, fear, and hope; but these emotions were kept in order and peace by original uprightness. This beautiful order was destroyed in the fall; the same passions remained, but their use was changed. Love for God degenerated into self-love, fear into evil, courage and hope into distrust. Man, instead of loving God, now hates Him. Christ said, "But I know you, that ye have not the love of God in you" (John 5:42). Reverential fear has deteriorated into evil courage against God. "The kings of the earth set themselves, and the rulers take counsel together, against the Lord, and against his anointed ..." (Ps. 2:2). Hope has degraded into unbelief. Our Saviour said, "Which of you convinceth me of sin? And if I say the truth, why do ye not believe me?" (John 8:46). Thus, the fall of man caused the soul to become a chaos that needed redemption.

Original uprightness was an essential part of Adam's human nature; it was the bridle that controlled the desires and actions of his nature. There are some who teach that Adam came forth perfect from the hand of the Creator and was subsequently clothed with original uprightness. This makes human nature a finished product apart from original uprightness. If Adam's nature was perfect before he possessed original uprightness, then it remained perfect after the loss of it. This cannot be true because *original sin is more than negative absence of original uprightness; it is positive corruption.*

Original uprightness consists of *positive* qualities. Without these man could not have answered the purpose of his creation. Adam and Eve heard the voice of the Lord God walking in the garden (Gen. 3:8). Here is an anthropomorphic (human form or characteristic) representation of fellowship between creature and Creator; this illustrates the ability of man's rational nature to understand something of the rational being of God as the latter chooses to reveal it. As man knows and loves finitely, so God knows and loves infinitely. God assigned Adam the *responsibility* of naming all the creatures of air, land, and sea (Gen. 1:20-25; 2:19,20). This presupposes rationality and scientific knowledge. Adam must have known something about the nature of all these creatures in order to name them. Man was God's deputy governor in the lower world, and this was an image of God's sovereignty. While man saw himself lord of the creatures, he must not forget that he was still God's subject. Moral duty is implicit in such an assignment, but the moral nature of man is more evident still in the command and prohibition concerning eating of the forbidden fruit (Gen 2:16,17). God made the beasts looking down toward the earth to show that their satisfaction comes from beneath; the erect posture of man's body shows that his satisfaction comes from above. The forbidden tree taught man his dependence on God; there was want even in Eden. The intellectual nature of man is usually designated as the image of God in the broader sense; the holy nature is the image of God in the narrower sense. The intellectual sense is never lost, even in hell; the holy nature was lost, even in Eden.

Man was created male and female; ". . . Male and female created he them" (Gen. 1:27). Woman was not a separate creation. The Bible presents her as differentiated from the male by being drawn from his side. Man had one thing peculiar to himself; namely, he had dominion over the woman. ". . . Thy desire shall be to thy husband, and he shall rule over thee" (Gen. 3:16). The woman is compelled to look to her husband for her desires, this is her dependence. As she lives under his authority, her dependence becomes submission. Her place therefore is secondary and dependent. The reason for this is because the woman was formed after and made for man. Paul said, "But I would have you know, that the head of every man is Christ; and the head of the woman is the man; and the head of Christ is God" (I Cor. 11:3). As the woman was to be in subjection to the man, so man must be in subjection to God. This was just another way God revealed to man that while he had dominion over the lower creatures, he must not forget that *he is under the absolute dominion of God.*

The original uprightness of Adam was mutable. If Adam had been unchangeably upright, he must be so either *by nature* or *by gift.* He could not be unchangeably upright by nature; that is proper to God alone and cannot be communicated to any of His creatures. If by gift, then no wrong was done him in withholding that which he could not desire. Adam, whose will was *free,* chose not the will of God but his own will. If Adam who was in a state of original uprightness chose evil, what about man in a state of depravity? Thus, we understand that created uprightness is capable of sinning because it is finite. The infinite God cannot create infinity; therefore, His creation is inferior to Himself.

Adam was left to himself and fell. If man in created uprightness did not stand, how shall man in his depraved condition stand? The fall came about through his wife whom Satan beguiled. Satan knew that a temptation coming through his wife would be less suspected. He persuaded Eve by *subtracting* from, *adding* to *and altering* the

Word of God. This was Satan's masterpiece to weaken faith in what God said. When Eve was brought to the place of distrust, she yielded to the temptation. Satan broke over the hedge of original uprightness where it was the *weakest* (I Pet. 3:7; I Tim. 2:14). He knew he could more easily reach Adam through Eve than by going directly to him. This same approach is revealed in the sin of Ahab. "... Ahab, which did sell himself to work wickedness in the sight of the Lord, whom Jezebel his wife stirred up" (I Kings 21:25). Satan's method has never changed.

Adam and Eve sought out many inventions (Eccl. 7:29). Not only were they together in sin, but the ways of their sin (inventions) were many. Among the inventions of our first parents, there were *many excuses and pleas sought out to justify their conduct and to make them appear unfortunate rather than criminal.* This proves that man was the cause of his fall. Man's fall could never take away God's right to command obedience and to punish in the case of disobedience.

It was Adam's fault that he did not do as God commanded. God made a covenant with Adam to show His sovereignty over all His creatures. Pharaoh made Joseph chief ruler of his kingdom, but he said, "... only in the throne will I be greater than thou" (Gen. 41:40). God dealt with Adam in the same manner. He gave him dominion over all His lower creation. God knew that Adam would transgress, but that was no reason for not giving the law. Shall laws cease to be made because some will break them? God ordained Adam's transgression to manifest the riches of His grace. This was done by sending Christ Who would keep the law by an obedient life and pay the penalty of the broken law by His voluntary death. Though man is a little lower than the angels (to whom he is inferior in nature though superior in destiny), it is a mark of extreme condescension that God visits him in Christ. Man's original creation was of the earth earthy in contrast to his recreation (regeneration) in Christ (I Cor. 15:45-49). Consequently, the Christian "... is renewed in knowledge after the image of him that created him" (Col. 3:10). The righteous state of the Christian is the uncreated righteousness of God, and in this gracious state he can never fall. Where is the foolish person who would exchange the uncreated righteousness of Christ for the created uprightness of Adam?

Original sin is *positive* as well as *negative.* It is true that original purity has been lost, and the nature has been defiled. Original sin has contaminated our nature; it has been turned into a depraved spring, and from this spring flows all kinds of sinful acts. When the soul of Adam *died (not cessation of existence but separation of existence),* it became *passive* as far as good was concerned. It was incapable of any good, and *active* to all evil. Original sin is called the *old man* because man's original beauty has been destroyed. It is called the *law of sin* because of its power to bind its subject to sin (Eph. 4:22; Rom. 7:25). Depraved man has not only the *love of sin* to draw him but the *law of sin* to drive him. Solomon said, "Foolishness is bound up in the heart of a child; but the rod of correction shall drive it far from him" (Prov. 22:15). It is soon seen in the child which way the bias of his heart lies, for "Even a child is known by his doings . . . " (Prov. 20:11). Do not the children of Adam, before they can go alone, follow their father's footsteps? The baby first puts everything into its mouth—*lust of the flesh;* it wants everything it sees—*lust of the eyes;* it desires to show off—*the pride of life.* What a vast amount of pride, ambition, sinful curiosity, vanity, wilfulness, and averseness to good appear in children! As soon as they leave infancy, there is necessity of using the rod of correction to drive away the foolishness in their actions. If grace does not intervene, children will grow to be Ishmaels—"wild men" (Gen. 16:12). The rod can only drive foolishness from their actions, but it takes the grace of God to drive it out of their hearts.

Adam is a representative man. While he stood, we stood; when he fell, we fell. The Scripture takes particular care to point out that Adam communicates his image to his posterity. "And Adam lived an hundred and thirty years, and begat a son in his own likeness, after his image, and called his name Seth" (Gen. 5:3). Compare this verse with Genesis 5:1: " . . . In the day that God created man, in the likeness of God made he him." The difference between man *created* and *begotten* is revealed. Man was created after God's likeness; the descendants of Adam are begotten in the likeness of Adam who had fallen from original uprightness into a state of corruption. This was original sin. David said, ". . . In sin did my mother conceive me" (Ps. 51:5). Having sinned, Adam became mortal and begat mortals; for Paul said, ". . . In Adam all die . . ." (I Cor. 15:22).

The principle of representation teaches that all men without exception *sinned in Adam* (Rom. 5:12; I Cor. 15:22). This original sin, therefore, was *imputed* to all of Adam's descendants as a natural consequence of their involvement in Adam's act. This means that all of us sinned and are held guilty with Adam in original sin. No person can merit the penalty of death in another unless *with* and *in* that person he has sinned. It is not sufficient to say that all die in Adam because we receive from him original sin. Could we not for the same reason say that we die in our parents from whom we directly derived sin? The Bible never states that we die in our parents, but in Adam all die (I Cor. 15:22). This principle is illustrated in the case of Levi who is said to have " ... payed tithes in Abraham. For *he was yet in the loins of his father ... "* (Heb. 7:9,10). Thus, the imputation of Adam's sin is *real* (the reckoning to one of that which is antecedently his) and *immediate* (preceded man's corruption and is reckoned to be the cause of corruption).

The relation of a person and his ego must be considered if we are to understand the working of the depraved nature. The *ego* refers to the entire man—body and mind. The corrupt condition of fallen nature could not be excited to do things if there were no personal ego. The unbalanced powers of the soul cause the darkening of the understanding (Eph. 4:18), and the loss of a free will enables the evil passions to be aroused (Rom. 1:24-28). The unbalanced powers of the soul and the loss of free will could not result in sin if man's personal ego were not affected by their workings. Sin puts its own mark upon this corrupt and depraved nature *only when the ego turns away from God. The unbelieving ego is identified with the old depraved nature.*

The old nature is not changed in regeneration, but an entirely new man is implanted. *Regeneration affects only our person.* Old nature in believers is condemned, but not saved (Rom. 8:3). The principle of grace, which is formed in the heart in regeneration, bears the likeness of Christ; therefore, *the believing ego is identified with the new man.*

We are now in a position to better understand Christ's human nature. If Jesus Christ had been born a human person by the will of man, he would have had an ego turned away from God. *But He was not born a human person;* He took a human nature that was conceived by the Holy Spirit, and this was not by the will of man. *Neither could there be in Him an ego turned away from God, nor the weakness of His human nature be a sinful weakness.* He was given the Holy Spirit without measure to strengthen the weakness of His Impeccable human nature. God the Spirit transformed (not regenerated) Christ's human nature into a glorified nature by the power of the resurrection.

The human nature of Christ had no subsistence but in the Second Person of the Godhead. This raises the human nature of Christ to an infinitely higher level than man's nature. His human nature had a glorious subsistence. That which Christ did in His human nature was the performance of God. There was *but one ego in Jesus Christ.* The union of the two natures in one Person made Him the Son of God and the Son of Man in the same Person.

Was the original guilt of Adam imputed to Christ? If it was, then Christ, like all other men, was involved in Adam's sin and guilt. It was necessary, for the purpose of manifestation, that Christ become truly human; but impossible for Him, in His conception, to partake of Adam's sin and guilt. If guilt had been imputed to Christ at His conception, there would have been both involvement in Adam's sin and defilement of His Person. This would not only have made impossible the union of God and man, but also His substitutionary sacrifice. He would have had to die for His own sins, justly His because of imputation, rather than dying willingly as the *sinless one* Who voluntarily took upon Himself the judgment for sin. Adam's guilt is imputed to his posterity, but Jesus Christ is not a descendant of Adam; He existed before Adam. Jesus Christ does not stand under Adam as his head, but He is the Head of Adam (I Cor. 11:3). Does this not reveal the evil of the doctrine of peccability?

CHRIST'S HUMAN BODY

The Temple of Christ's Body came from a Spirit-separated place in the womb of Mary (Luke 1:35; Heb. 10:5). The primitive priest, with his measuring line, would go into the field and measure off a choice portion of ground for erection of the temple; so the Holy Spirit, with His power of separation, went into the womb of Mary and selected a place for the erection of the Temple of Christ's Body. Not only was this Body *negatively sinless;* it was from the first *positively full of the Holy Spirit.* The Son of God took to Himself that sacred site in the womb of the virgin, and within it He began to build such a holy life that He speaks of it as the "Temple of his Body" (John 2:21).

When Christ visited Jerusalem at the time of the passover, He found the temple the center of carnal activities (John 2:13-17). The passover had degenerated into the Jews' passover. God's house had become a house of merchandise, and this angered the Son of God. The Saviour entered the temple and saw His Father's house invaded by religious hypocrites. "Now when he was in Jerusalem at the passover, in the feast day, many believed in his name, when they saw the miracles which he did. But Jesus did not commit himself unto them, because he knew all men, And needed not that any should testify of man: for he knew what was in man" (John 2:23-25). His knowledge of man was not by report—but by Divine wisdom. Christ's omniscience should cause hypocrites to tremble and Christians to be steadfast.

The Lord did not overstep the bounds of His authority by cleansing the temple. Since the temple was God's meeting place with men, it was to be cleansed from all foreign substance. It must not be desecrated. Christ's disciples remembered that it was written, " . . . The zeal of *thine house* hath eaten me up" (John 2:17). *Holy zeal* is concerned with God's honor and man's salvation, but *there can be no salvation of men where the honor of God is not asserted.* The word *zeal* is described as a boiling heart, a heart boiling over with the intense heat of its own affections, passions, and emotions. Thus, the holy zeal of Christ *"ate Him up."* This is an arresting expression. His all-consuming zeal led Him to remove from the temple the *"zeal which was not according to knowledge"* (Rom. 10:2).

Zeal which is not according to Divine knowledge dishonors God; therefore, it must be removed from the place where God's honor is maintained.

Does the zeal of God's house (the church) eat us up? Is not the church, the place where the glory of God is found (Eph. 3:21), to be kept clean from every unholy zeal? There is a zeal which has the appearance of being for the Lord, but it stems wholly from carnal and selfish motives. "Come," said King Jehu, "and see my zeal for the Lord" (II Kings 10:16). But all the time Jehu's zeal was for himself and not for the Lord at all. He was zealous for the things that would make him appear great in the eyes of men. Paul, before his salvation from sin, said, ". . . being more exceedingly *zealous* of the traditions of my fathers" (Gal. 1:13,14). *Zeal without knowledge* has been the strength and animating demon of every active evil. This is revealed in the failure of traditionalists to turn from their human traditions to the pure revelation of God's truth (Mark 7:1-9). Christians are a priestly people (I Pet. 2:5-10) called to keep the temple of God pure upon the earth. Many religionists bring their money, sports, and traditions to church; consequently, they are " . . . almost in all evil in the midst of the congregation and assembly" (Prov. 5:14). The great sin of the Corinthians was their failure to discern the Lord's Body (I Cor. 11:29), and this heinous sin is committed today by many.

The authority of Christ was questioned by the Jews who saw Him cleanse the temple. They asked, "What sign showest thou?" He answered and said unto them, "Destroy this temple, and in three days I will raise it up" (John 2:19). The Pharisees did not understand this saying. Christ did not refer to the cleansed temple; the zeal of which consumed Him. The temple which had been cleansed was shown to be a figure of something greater. Our Lord proclaimed Himself to be the antitype, the new Temple in which the fulness of the Godhead dwelt bodily. The Saviour had the authority to cleanse the temple in Jerusalem and to raise up a *Temple which men could destroy but not construct.* Christ, therefore, said, "No man taketh it from me, but I lay it down of myself. I have power to lay it down, and I have power to take it again . . . " (John 10:18). Our Lord announced His death by the *figure* of a destroyed and rebuilt temple. His enemies would destroy the Temple of His Body, but the resurrection thereof would be performed by Himself.

The resurrection would prove Christ's authority for cleansing the temple in Jerusalem and demonstrate Who He was.

In the perfection of Christ's Body there was the vigor of perfect health. His Body was capable of pain and weariness, but not of sickness; it was capable of death, but not subject to it. The Body of the *sinless Saviour could not know corruption* either in life or death. Corruption is the consequence of the fall; hence, it pertains only to those who share in it. No one could ever say that the Holy One of God shared in the fall. Peter, in his exaltation of Christ on the day of Pentecost, said, "Therefore did my heart rejoice, and my tongue was glad; moreover also my flesh shall rest in hope: Because thou wilt not leave my soul in hell, neither wilt thou suffer thine Holy One to see corruption ... He seeing this before spake of the resurrection of Christ ... " (Acts 2:26,27,31).

During *"the days of Christ's flesh,"* He prayed, hungered, slept, and rested because He was "the man approved by God" (Acts 2:22). We must not diminish the glory of Christ's Deity, nor should we take from His humanity. To do so would destroy our Lord's sacrificial death and glorious resurrection. Thus, we would have no gospel which would result in no glorious resurrection. There were times when His days were so full that He had no opportunity to partake of bodily food (Mark 3:20; 6:31). On one occasion after a long journey, He sat weary and thirsty on a well; but even in weariness and hunger He labored on, refreshed and comforted by the joy of doing the Father's will (John 4:34). He was not as Moses and Jeremiah, pleading inability to speak God's message; on the contrary, He said, " ... Lo, I come to do thy will, O God ... " (Heb. 10:9), and " .. I do always those things that please him" (John 8:29). He, therefore, passed through all the experiences of men—*sin and sickness excepted.*

The "Temple of Christ's Body" is *the appointed place* where God meets men in mercy. "To wit, that God was in Christ, reconciling the world unto himself, not imputing their trespasses unto them ... " (II Cor. 5:19). This Temple, like the tabernacle in the wilderness, was more glorious *within* than *without.* Isaiah described the *outside* of the Temple by saying, ". . . he hath no form nor comeliness; and when we shall see him, there is no beauty that we should desire him" (Is. 53:2). As the priests of Israel beheld the beauty *in the tabernacle,* so Christians (a royal priesthood) are the people who behold the beauty *in the Lord Jesus Christ*. The religious Jews saw only the outside of the Saviour; therefore, they desired to kill Him, for they saw no beauty *in* Him. Christians, however, see *in* Him the beauty of grace and truth and say, "My Lord and my God."

The Temple of Christ's Body *was offered once as a sacrifice for sin* (Heb. 10:10,14). Why does the Holy Spirit emphasize Christ's Body rather than His Soul? If Jesus Christ suffered in His Body only, He would have been a redeemer of bodies only; but his *Soul* also was made an offering (Is. 53:10), and this was to provide redemption for souls. Emphasis on the *Body* was to make plain the fact that redemption was to be accomplished by death. Since the Soul cannot die, *redemption must be accomplished in the Body which could die.* His Body, however, was not subject to death as our bodies. Therefore, our salvation was accomplished by Christ's Body going *through death* (Heb. 2:14)—an experience impossible among men.

The Body of Christ *sanctifies the believer forever* (Heb. 10:10). The word *once* and the word *forever* stand or fall together. The *once* of Christ's work is the secret of its being *forever*. The propitiation for sin was so complete that God now remembers the sin no more forever; this indicates that He has forgiven the sinner. Forgiveness signifies that God *forgets away* every sin. Forgetting in the Divine mind is an attribute, but in the human mind it is a defect. Consequently, *God never illustrates His Divine forgetfulness by human representations;* but by similitudes taken from His own creation. "As far as the east is from the west, so far hath he removed our transgressions from us" (Ps. 103:12). "I have blotted out, as a thick cloud, thy transgressions, and, as a cloud, thy sins ... " (Is. 44:22). God never uses a human illustration of forgiveness because a human being is incapable of forgiving as God forgives. Man understands forgiveness to imply something he can understand, but it is of such magnitude that it demands the Holy Spirit to enable him to comprehend that which is made his through grace. When this is realized by the believer, the conscience becomes perfect. "For the law having a shadow of good things to come, and not the very image of the things, can never with those sacrifices which they offered year by year continually make the comers thereunto perfect... For by one offering he hath perfected for ever them that are sanctified" (Heb. 10:1, 14).

The resurrection of Christ's Body is God's attestation of the fact that He is Divine. "Concerning his Son Jesus Christ our Lord, which was made of the seed of David according to the flesh; and declared to be the Son of God with power, according to the spirit of holiness, by the resurrection from the dead" (Rom. 1:3,4). The One Who had power to lay down His life had power to take it again. Not only was His resurrection the proof of His Deity, but it guaranteed the resurrection of our bodies. " ... Christ the first-fruits; afterward they that are Christ's at his coming" (I Cor. 15:23). " ... In my flesh shall I see God" (Job 19:26). Job had no hope of a restoration to temporal prosperity; nevertheless, he spoke in the most confident manner of his resurrection to eternal glory. If he could see his Redeemer apart from the flesh in the spiritual realm, there would be no need for his Saviour to stand in His Body at the latter day upon the earth. John said, " ... When he shall appear, we shall be like him; for we shall see him as he is" (I John 3:2). As He will appear in His glorified Body, so shall we appear before Him in our glorified bodies.

CHRIST'S HUMAN SOUL

The Lord Jesus Christ had not only a human body but also a human soul. " ... My *soul* is exceeding sorrowful, even unto death ... " (Matt. 26:38). "Yet it pleased the Lord to bruise him; he hath put him to grief: When thou shalt make his *soul* an offering for sin" (Is 53:10). It was necessary that the human nature of the Saviour be complete, *with the contamination of the fall excluded.* Since Jesus Christ was not included in the covenant under which our first parents stood, He could not be accused of that guilt which attended the violation of it. Thus, He became the perfect sacrifice for sin.

We must distinguish the soul of Christ from the soul of man in order to understand the nature of Christ's human soul. *Soul is the immaterial part of man.* Something more took place in the creation of man than in that of the beasts. God did not breathe into beasts the breath of lives; therefore, man has a link with God which they do not have. Breath is not the soul; it denotes the *manner of its infusion and means of its continuation.* It has been said that the soul was created in the infusion and infused in creation. When God breathed into the nostrils of man the breath of *life*—lives, he became a *living soul* (Gen. 2:7). Hebrew scholars say the word life should be plural—lives. Man has more than one life, this and that which is to come. " ... having the promise of the life that now is, and of that which is to come" (I Tim. 4:8).

Why is man called a living soul rather than a living spirit? The point of contrast is between men and angels. Angels are spirits; they are never called souls. Man, however, made a little lower than the angels is called a soul. That which links man with inferior creatures is that which distinguishes him from the angels. Thus, *the soul is the subject of personal life,* and *the spirit is the principle.*

The soul has a never-ending existence, but it is not eternal. That which is eternal has no beginning nor ending; therefore, eternality is applicable to none but God. "The eternal God is thy refuge, and underneath are the everlasting arms ... " (Deut. 33:27). The never-ending existence of the soul had a beginning, but it has no ending. It cannot cease when once it has been created. As the eternity of God exhibits the greatness of God, so the never-ending existence of the soul displays the greatness of the soul.

The expression, *the immortality of the soul* is without Scriptural foundation. Such a statement can be very misleading. We should not give the enemies of the never-ending existence of the soul any ground for argument by using wrong terminology. *Mortality* and *immortality* are both physical terms. Christ is the one exception to the universal program in which either incorruption or immortality is attained. Though he died, He did not see corruption. His present estate is not that of incorruption but immortality. "For thou wilt not leave my soul in hell; neither wilt thou suffer thine Holy One to see corruption" (Ps. 16:10; Acts 2:27). Paul describes Christ's bodily estate: "Who only hath immortality, dwelling in the light which no man can approach unto; whom no man hath seen, nor can see: to whom be honour and power everlasting. Amen" (I Tim. 6:16). Christ has entered into His transformed immortal body; believers await the resurrection for their glorified bodies. This, however, has no bearing on the present redemption of the soul.

Immortality is immunity from death. Adam, who was made a living soul, did not possess immortality. He was warned of death for eating the forbidden fruit. *What is death?* Death is not ceasing to exist; it is existence out of harmony with or separation from God. *Death, therefore, is not cessation of existence but separation of existence.* This condition has passed to the whole human race. Man is alive to the world, but dead to God (Eph. 2:1; John 5:24). The believer is immune from spiritual death; nevertheless, physically speaking, he has not yet immortality. Immortality will be experienced by the believer when Christ returns (I Cor. 15). The unbeliever, however, will exist both spiritually and physically in alienation and separation from God for all eternity. "...This is the second death" (Rev. 20:14). Sin is that which makes death so terrible, for the sting of death is sin (I Cor. 15:56). If sin in the *retrospect* be the sting of death, what must sin in the *prospect* be? (Rev. 22:11).

The soul is the connecting link between spirit and body. The spirit is the higher part, the *thinker;* soul is the *feeler.* "He (Christ) *sighed* deeply in his spirit..." (Mark 8:12). The word *sighed* is a bodily and not a mental phenomenon. This language no more confounds soul and spirit than it does body and spirit. Christ's sigh was caused by His spirit discerning the moral character of those who desired to see a sign from heaven. Soul and spirit are not always interchangeable terms. The soul, not the spirit, is said to be lost. The Spirit bears witness with our spirit—not our soul (Rom. 8:16). When no technical distinctions are in view, the Bible is dichotomous; otherwise, it is trichotomous. (See Matt. 10:28; Acts 2:31; Rom. 8:10; I Cor. 5:3; 6:20; 7:34; Eph. 4:4; James 2:26; I Peter 2:11.) The same function may be ascribed to either the soul or the spirit; the departed are sometimes mentioned as soul and sometimes spirit. Body and spirit may be separated; soul and body may be separated, but soul and spirit can only be distinguished.

Much controversy rages over the derivation and perpetuation of the soul of man. It is imperative that we penetrate this cloud of controversy since the derivation of Christ's human soul is to be considered. The two theories which have been engaged in battle for centuries are known as *Creationism* and *Traducianism*.

Traducianism teaches that both soul and body are propagated by human generation. This theory does not deny the Creation hypothesis, but it does deny that it takes place each time a person is born. This system believes the person is not propagated in parts, but as a whole. Man is no longer created by supernatural power; he is derived out of an existing human substance by means of natural law and Divine supervision.

The sinlessness of Christ poses a problem to the Traducianists. They say there is no problem if the miraculous conception be embraced. Some Traducianists teach that Christology must include justification as well as sanctification because sin is guilt as well as pollution. Thus, they believe the human nature of Christ was peccable, but in union with Deity the person was impeccable. Their conclusion is that the *Logos* could not unite with a nature that had not previously been delivered from both the condemnation and corruption of sin. Thus, the justification of the flesh by the Spirit (I Tim. 3:16), like that of Old Testament believers, was proleptical (anticipation) in view of the future atoning death of Christ.

This view of the Traducianists concerning the peccability of Christ's human nature and its justification and sanctification is dangerous theology. What are the meanings of justification and sanctification as they are used in reference to Christ? Only in our understanding of these two subjects, and their use in connection with Christ, can we have a Biblical view of His human nature.

Justification is a legal term used to designate the acceptance of anyone as righteous in the sight of God. Justification does not *make* a person righteous; it *declares* him righteous. A wicked man may be justified (pronounced guiltless), and a just (guiltless) person may be condemned, but they are abomination to the Lord (Prov. 17:15). The sinner is justified (declaratively) on the ground of the Impeccable Saviour's righteousness, but *how is Christ justified?* "And without controversy great is the mystery of godliness: God was manifest in the flesh, *justified in the Spirit* ... " (I Tim. 3:16). The world had a false conception of the Lord Jesus. Even the religious world did not believe Him to be the eternal Son of God. The chief priests mocked Him, and the scribes said, "He saved others; himself he cannot save. If he be the King of Israel, let him now come down from the cross, and we will believe him. He trusted in God; let him deliver him now, if he will have him: for *he said, I am the Son of God*" (Matt. 27:42,43). The Son of God *appeared to them* but a poor, despised, and debased man. It did not matter, however, *what he appeared to be in the flesh* (the likeness of sinful flesh) ; *He was justified in the Spirit.* Justification in the life of the sinner supposes guilt, but it could never suppose this in the human nature of Christ. Christ's justification in (by) the Spirit cleared Him from all false conceptions. As wisdom is justified of all her children (Luke 7:35), so the Son of God is declared just by all who have received the revelation of heaven (Matt. 16:13-17). His human nature was never contaminated by the fall of man.

Sanctification means *to set apart.* The word is used in a twofold way: *Positional,* separation to God's presence; *Practical,* the manifestation of Christ in the life of the person separated to God. The first is absolute (I Cor. 1:2; Heb. 10:10,14) ; the second is progressive (John 17:17; I Thess. 4:3-7). The latter is exercised in the power of the Spirit; Christ within produces Christ without.

Since some Traducianists believe that Christ's human nature was peccable, then it is natural for them to say that His human nature was delivered (positionally sanctified) from pollution as well as guilt. But where does it say that His human nature was delivered from guilt and corruption? It is nowhere found in the Sacred Book. Christ did say, "And for their sakes I sanctify myself, that they also might be sanctified through the truth" (John

17:19). This statement meant no more than Christ *setting Himself apart* as a sacrifice acceptable and well-pleasing in the sight of God for the salvation of the elect (John 17:2,6,9,11,12,24). The Holy Spirit did enter the womb of Mary and sanctify (set apart) that part of her which would produce the human nature of our Saviour; therefore, that *holy thing* which was born of her was the Son of God. The Spirit, therefore, purified Mary; not the human nature of Christ.

Creationism teaches that the soul of each person is immediately created by God and is joined to the body either at conception or birth or sometime between. Thus, the body is generated by the parents, but the soul is the immediate creation of God. From the standpoint of Traducianism, this presents great difficulty as to the process by which these souls became defiled. The Traducianist believes this theory makes God the author of evil.

Can that which is immaterial (the soul) be brought forth by the material (the body)? Creationism does not believe that man does what animals do: generate the whole of their species. Whatever is generated by man is subject to death, but the soul has a never-ceasing existence.

Can God create a soul impotent of that which is good without His credibility being challenged? Do not the Scriptures teach that everything God creates is good? *Yes and No.* What kind of double talk is this? It is not double talk! The *original creation* of everything was pronounced good (Gen. 1). But God through Isaiah said, "I am the Lord, and there is none else, there is no God beside me ... I form the light, and *create darkness:* I make peace, and *create evil:* I the Lord do all these things" (Is. 45:5,7). Both *darkness* and *evil* are said to be *of God.* How can this be? Darkness, whether it be natural or judicial, is deprivation of light. Has not the Sovereign God the right to deprive some of light if He so chooses? The evil is *not the evil of sin,* but *the evil of punishment for sin* by various judgments which God sends upon people.

Let it be observed, therefore, that God can create a soul impotent of what is good without any impeachment of His perfection. The law for the propagation of mankind was given to man before his fall. Adam, in the fall, defiled his whole nature and that of his posterity; for they sinned in him. Is it reasonable, now, that because man has departed from his obedience to the law of God that

God should depart from His original law respecting man's generation? Nature itself does not do that. For example, a man steals a quantity of seed and sows them in his field. Nature proceeds according to its own laws and causes the seed to sprout, grow, and come to fruition. Is nature unjust by giving a good crop from stolen seed? No, nor is God unjust to continue giving men their souls even though generation might be unlawfully begotten in adultery or fornication.

Original sin comes not to the soul alone, nor by the body alone; it comes from the union of soul and body. God may create a soul with all its natural powers and properties, and these without infusing any sinfulness or inclination to sin. God as Creator is not to be thought of only in part, but as the active Creator in man's history (Job 10:8; 33:4; Is. 43:15; Ps. 102:18). Creationism, therefore, has no problem with Christ's human soul; and sufficient has been said for the soul of man.

We have seen something about what the soul *is;* we shall now consider what the soul *does* through its members, senses, and passions. The good or evil of these things is determined not by these things in themselves, but by the principle that controls them. In the Christian they are controlled by the principle of grace, but in the sinner by the power of Satan.

As the body has many members, so does the soul. The soul has understanding (Eph. 1:18; Luke 24:45), conscience (Rom. 2:15; I Tim. 3:9), judgment (I Cor. 5:12), mind (Titus 1:15; II Tim. 1:7), memory (II Pet. 3:1), affections (Col. 3:2), and will (John 1:13).

As the body has senses, so does the soul. The soul can see (Eph. 1:18; Job 35:14), hear (John 5:24; Job 4:12,13; 33:16), taste (I Pet. 2:2,3), smell (S. of S. 1:3; 5:5,13), and feel (Ps. 38:1-8).

The soul also has passions; they are: love (S. of S. 8:6,7), hatred (Ps. 97:10), joy (I Cor. 13:6), fear (Matt. 10:28; Phil. 3:12), grief (Ps. 119:158), and anger (Eph. 4:26).

A sick body is a burden to the soul, but "a wounded spirit who can bear?" (Prov. 18:14). Death, for the sinner, does not remove this burden; the soul must have the body for a burden, and the body must have the soul for a burden. This is terrifying; but do not forget that the members, senses, and passions of the soul will constitute a tremendous burden of punishment. When you add to this burden the burden of God's wrath, it is indescribable—burden upon burden—infinite punishment.

Jesus Christ possessed, in His human soul, the same members, senses, and passions we possess; but *His were absolutely perfect.* They were absolutely perfect because His soul was Impeccable. In body and soul He grew up before the Lord as a "tender plant" (Is. 53:2). The Lord of nature is seen conformed to the law of nature. He bowed before the storm like a tender shoot, but was not uprooted by the tempest. That which is absolutely perfect cannot be uprooted. The Impeccable soul of Christ was troubled. "Now is my soul troubled; and what shall I say?" (John 12:27). This was no sinful weakness. Man is like a puddle when troubled, but Christ is as clear water in a clean vessel. As clean water in a vessel remains clean no matter how often stirred, so the Person of Christ in an Impeccable body and soul remained unchanged in character no matter how much He was troubled.

CHRIST'S HUMAN GROWTH

Luke reveals that he had a good understanding of the beginning of our Lord's earthly life. He had seen and interrogated the most trusted eye-witnesses of our Lord's human growth from infancy to manhood. "And the child grew, and waxed strong in spirit, filled with wisdom: and the grace of God was upon Him" (Luke 2:40). "And Jesus increased in wisdom and stature, and in favour with God and man" (Luke 2:52). There was nothing supernatural about the growth and development of Christ's body; we read the same thing concerning John the Baptist (Luke 1:80). However, there was something supernatural about His response to everything that was honest, just, and pure. There was never the same degree of response in the sons of men; only the eternal Son of God could give such response. Foolishness is bound up in the heart of every natural child of Adam's race (Prov. 22:15); nevertheless, this Child was not the natural but the supernatural Child of the Holy Spirit. There was no foolishness in His Impeccable heart.

The Child grew for God cannot grow. The body which God prepared grew and waxed strong. It was not formed from the dust of the earth, but in the womb of the virgin. It was necessary for Him to experience every part of humanity from childhood to manhood. There is not a stage in human life in which God has not been glorified. Human perfection was seen in Jesus Christ; He came into the world veiled in "that Holy Thing" (Luke 1:35). Adam could not have been sympathetic with the feelings of a child, for he never was a child; this could not be said of Jesus Christ.

Christ had, by necessity, all wisdom and power from the beginning. *He subjected Himself to the laws of human development.* In Infancy He exhibited a perfect Infant; in Childhood, a perfect Child; in Youth, a perfect Youth; and in Manhood, a perfect Man. A perfect bud unfolded into a perfect flower. Thus, at each stage of development He was displaying larger measures of that perfect wisdom which was in Him from the beginning. He was "filled with wisdom," for wisdom is the principal thing (Prov. 4:7). It is not said that He was filled with knowledge or learning though all that would be true in His advancement of wisdom. Knowledge too often puffs up (I Cor. 8:1), but wisdom always edifies. Everything He learned descended into His Impeccable heart, and out of His heart were the issues of His Impeccable growth and life. The word *increased* (Luke 2:52) is better translated *advanced or progressed;* it is a word derived from pioneers who cut down trees in the pathway of an advancing army. He was always "filled with wisdom," but *it developed in His experience* as He grew in stature.

How can He Who was eternally filled with wisdom increase in wisdom? How can that which is absolutely full be made to hold more? Does not development imply imperfection passing into perfection? There are two ideas of growth and development. The first is *development through antagonism,* and this is what we as Christians experience because of the evil nature (Rom. 7:15-25; Gal. 5:17). But there is another kind of development, and it is the *development of a perfect nature limited by time.* The plant is perfect when it is a green shoot above the earth; it is all that it can be at that time. It is more perfect as the plant is adorned with leaves and branches; it is all that it can be at that time. The plant reaches its *full perfection* when the bud opens into a flower. Such was the development of Christ. There was no antagonism in His development because there was no evil nature in Him. When the Scripture says, "... the grace of God was upon him" (Luke 2:40), the Spirit expressed something not internal but external. We are not to think of *grace* in its ordinary use. We need grace for salvation, but He needed no salvation. The idea expressed is the good pleasure of God upon Him.

The *natural growth* of the human nature of Christ represents the *spiritual growth* of the Christian. There are *two kinds of incompleteness:* that which is growing to completeness, and that which comes from the presence of an opposing force. We may say of the first that a child is a perfect human being when all adjustments are right in his various stages of growth. He is not a perfect human being, however, in the sense of growth and maturity. The effort of a child to perform that which can be accomplished only by an adult is not in the same category as failure through wilful disobedience. The limitation of the child's growing power prevents his succeeding. The other kind of incompleteness comes from an opposing force, something which makes man say, "I will not." That opposing force is the Adamic nature. No incompleteness in that sense is found in Jesus Christ (Luke 2:40,52), for there was no opposing force in His Impeccable nature. As there was a birth and growth of the God-Man in the Person of Jesus Christ, so there must be a birth and growth of Christ in the souls of the elect. The first is a mystery (I Tim. 3:16); the second is also a mystery (Col. 1:27). Thus these two mysteries stand or fall together.

The earthly life of our Lord is divided into three periods: (1) from birth to the age of twelve; (2) from the age of twelve to His public manifestation; and (3) from His public manifestation to His death on the cross. It is perplexing to many that there should be so little said about the Saviour during the first thirty years of His earthly life. All growth is silent; therefore, God built His Temple without the sound of a hammer. His spiritual temple is also built without a great demonstration of noise and power.

We must never overlook the fact that the righteousness which Jesus Christ wrought out for us was a unit. It began at Bethlehem's manger and was consummated at Calvary. What our Lord did as a Child was as meritorious as what He did when He was a full grown Man. He was the Lamb without blemish and spot Who was offered upon the cross for our redemption. You cannot separate His vicarious death from His Impeccable life, nor His Impeccable life from His meritorious death. They both stand or fall together.

The first Adam was made in the likeness of God; the Second Adam was made in the likeness of sinful flesh. Had Christ come in power and great glory, there would have been no perfection of power through weakness (II Cor. 12:9). God proved to the world that He is stronger than men in all their strength (I Cor. 1:25). God will not permit *little* or *weak* things vilified. Isaiah had the honor of prophesying the Saviour's birth, and Micah the place of birth. "Therefore the Lord himself shall give you a sign; Behold, a virgin shall conceive, and bear a son . . ." (Is. 7:14). "But thou, Bethlehem Ephratah, though thou be little among the thousands of Judah, yet out of thee shall he come forth unto me that is to be ruler in Israel; whose goings forth have been from of old, from everlasting" (Micah 5:2). Here we see the *great* coming out of the *little;* the eternal Son coming out of Bethlehem. To despise little things is to despise Bethlehem and the *Holy Thing* that came out of Bethlehem. There are two *out-*

goings: the Son of God *before time;* the Son of Man *in the fulness of time.* No one can bring us to the eternity of glory but He Who came from an inhabited eternity (Is. 57:15).

Bethlehem speaks of humility. Both the place and the Person of the place confound the haughtiness of many who call themselves Christians. Christ's coming from Bethlehem was to recover man, and man could be recovered only by the opposite of that by which he perished. By pride man perished; by humility he is recovered. For man's pride, Christ was humbled; for man's exaltation, Christ was debased (Phil. 2:5-8).

The inn in Bethlehem was full the day of Christ's birth, but we can be sure that the stable where He was laid was not empty— God was there. "And she brought forth her firstborn son, and wrapped him in swaddling clothes, and laid him in a manger; because there was no room for them in the inn" (Luke 2:7). The inn was a *place where men were measured.* The best rooms were for the rich, and the common for the poor, but for Jesus Christ there was *no room.* There was no room in man's world for Christ Who was wholly cast upon God. Nor is there room now for the one who is wholly cast upon God. It is not dependent persons who get the best, but the independently rich who get the better things of this world. "For I was envious at the foolish, when I saw the prosperity of the wicked . . . Behold, these are the ungodly, who prosper in the world; they increase in riches" (Ps. 73:3,12).

The manger, not the Cathedral, *became a symbol of the place God blesses.* The grace that came into the world was found in the lowest place in the estimation of man. What is our sign now? The manger is gone, but the symbol remains. Humility is the place of God's presence; where there is no humility, there is no Christ.

True humility is fruitful; this is established by Bethlehem (little) Ephratah (fruitful). Scripture states, "There shall come forth a rod out of . . . Jesse . . . (Is. 11:1), out of it "a Branch" (Jer. 23:5), and from the branch the fruit of the virgin's womb (Luke 1:42). How great an Ephratah from such a small beginning! Bethlehem Ephratah means "humility the fruitful"; there is no repentance unless it is Ephratah: "bring forth fruits worthy of repentance" (Luke 3:8). Neither is there faith without "the work of faith", nor love without the "labor of love" (I Thess. 1:3). The place of our Lord's nativity was called Bethlehem Judah; this distinguishes it from Bethlehem in Zebulun (Josh. 19:15,16). Zebulun was by the sea; therefore, barren; Bethlehem Ephratah, however, was fruitful. Too much of the professed Christianity of our day is Bethlehem Zebulun (barren), and not Bethlehem Ephratah (fruitful). Those who deny the Impeccable growth and life of Jesus Christ are Bethlehem Zebulun (barren of spiritual life).

The circumcision and naming of the Holy Child is of great importance in His earthly life. He Who knew no sin was, typically in circumcision, made sin for us. He was in the world only eight days when He began to be numbered with transgressors. There was nothing unclean, either in His body or soul, for the knife of circumcision to cut away. No taint of sin ever touched this Holy Thing. He was never drawn away by lust because He had no lust within to be attracted to evil without. His circumcision was a shadow of good things to come. Whosoever is circumcised becomes a debtor to the whole law (Gal. 5:3). At His circumcision He signed a bond, as it were, and gave those few drops of blood as an earnest that He would shed all His blood for the debt of sin. He was given the name "Saviour" (Luke 2:21) at His circumcision.

The next recorded event in Christ's life was His visit to the Temple in Jerusalem. The first recorded statement that fell from His lips is stated here. Those words contain the purpose and mission of His earthly life. In the temple He discovered another home in which He was happier than the home of Joseph and Mary; it was there that He said, ". . . Wist ye not that I must be about my Father's business" (Luke 2:49). The eternal purpose, which was exalted above all human ties, filled His Being so that His whole nature was bent on its accomplishment. Our sin was the terrible business of God's Son. Here we have *an imperative must* which governs every step of the Saviour's earthly life. "I must work the works of him that sent me" (John 9:4). "The Son of Man must be lifted up" (John 3:14). "I must needs go through Samaria" (John 4:4). "I must abide at thy house" (Luke 19:5). "The Son of man must suffer many things, and be rejected of the elders and chief priests and scribes, and be slain, and be raised the third day" (Luke 9:22).

We now come to the last recorded incident in the first division of the Holy Child's life. He left the temple with His parents and came to Nazareth. He was subject unto them (Luke 2:51). How significant is this verse! God, Whom the angels obey, is subject to Joseph and Mary. The honor of parents comes after the honor of God in the order of the commandments, but in actual life the child obeys its parents before it obeys God. If this were not true the child could say, "Since I am not in subjection to God as His child, I do not have to be in subjection to you as my parents." At this very point parental subjection is about a thing of the past, and this is a sign of the last days. Where there is no fear of Divine authority, there is none for parental authority.

The main lesson our Lord would have us learn from His subjection to His parents is that a person is no more holy than he is relatively so. The word *relative* refers to the various relationships of life, and *holy* refers to love in all those relationships.

The years from twelve to thirty were silent. They are of immeasurable importance in any human life, and no less in the life of our Lord. There was in this period no boasting, hurry, nor impatience; but a quiet maturing power. There was orderly development because He is our perfect example (I Pet. 2:21) in every stage of development. There must be time for our preparation; we must learn before we teach, and obey before we command.

CHRIST'S BAPTISM

When Jesus Christ was baptized, the heavens were opened; and the Trinity attested His redeeming work. Spiritual ignorance would be manifested if we failed to notice the testimony of the Trinity in the baptism of Christ. "And Jesus, when he was baptized, went up straightway out of the water: and, lo, the heavens were opened unto him, and he saw the *Spirit of God* descending like a dove, and lighting upon him: And lo a *voice from heaven,* saying, This is my *beloved Son,* in whom I am well pleased" (Matt. 3:16,17). The heavens were opened that day because *the Man* was found in this world Who was *the suitable resting-place* for the Holy Spirit. As Noah's dove (Gen. 8:6-12) sought a resting place on earth, so the Holy Spirit sought a resting place here. This place was found in the Impeccable Son of Man. As the Father found delight in *the Son of Man,* so He finds delight in *every son of man who by regeneration becomes a "son of God"* (John 1:12). This is what Solomon saw: "Then I was by him, as one brought up with him: and I *was daily his delight,* rejoicing always before him; Rejoicing in the habitable part of his earth; and *my delights were with the sons of men"* (Prov. 8:30,31).

John the Baptist was sent to bear witness of the Light (John 1:6-8). His birth was second only to that of the Saviour in its mystery and grace. There is no mention of John from the time of his circumcision till he is heard preaching in the wilderness "... Repent ye: for the kingdom of heaven is at hand ..." (Matt. 3:2). He bridged the gap between the old and new covenants. The object of all prophecy, the purpose of all parts of the law (moral, judicial, and ceremonial), the end of all sacrifices, and the desire of all nations was at hand. This is He ". . . of whom Moses in the law, and the prophets, did write, Jesus of Nazareth, the son of Joseph" (John 1:45). John was the morning star ushering in the Son of God, but destined to fade in the glory of Him Who is the Light of the world. Therefore, he said, "He must increase, but I must decrease" (John 3:30). This is the spirit of every Christain who glorifies Christ in his life.

John the Baptizer came with the *"baptism of repentance"* (Matt. 3:11). Those who submitted to his baptism were taking the place of the guilty; they were accepting the sentence of God against themselves. "And all the people that heard him, and the publicans, *justified God,* being baptized with the baptism of John" (Luke 7:29). They justified God as the criminal does the judge when he acknowledges the justice of the sentence. John's baptism does *not mean that baptism preceded their repentance,* for the context proves that repentance was demanded as a prerequisite to baptism. Nevertheless, they went into the waters of the river confessing their sins.

The baptism of Christ was unique. The Lord Jesus was identifying Himself with the work He had come to fulfill. No person who existed before John, therefore, could follow Christ in His baptism. Christ came to earth to work out a righteousness and to satisfy the infinite claims of Divine justice. The Lord Jesus could not accomplish this literally by being baptized. Had He done so, He would have ascended directly to the right hand of God the Father as He came forth from the watery grave. There is some sense in which Christ fulfilled *"all righteousness'* by being baptized. All righteousness was *fulfilled figuratively,* but not literally in His baptism. This in no way takes from the fact that our Saviour had been fulfilling all manner of righteousness from youth. He had fulfilled ceremonial, moral, and legal righteousness. The Lord declared, through baptism, the climax of this righteousness which would be fulfilled in His death, burial, and resurrection. "But those things, which God before had shewed by the mouth of all his prophets, that Christ should suffer, *he hath so fulfilled"* (Acts 3:18). "For Christ is the end of the law for righteousness to every one that believeth" (Rom. 10:4). Our Lord, on more than one occasion, referred to His sufferings by the term baptism (Matt. 20:18-22; Luke 12:50).

What is the meaning of Matthew 3:15? "And Jesus answering said unto him, Suffer it to be so now: for *thus it becometh us to fulfil all righteousness* . . ." Some say Christ did this to show the importance of baptism in order for the sinner to fulfill all righteousness. This is the heresy of baptismal regeneration. Sinners are not only destitute of righteousness in their unregenerate state, but equally incapable of fulfilling the righteousness which God requires. All righteousness, therefore, is fulfilled not by sinful man; but by the Persons of the Godhead.

This righteousness of Christ is more than the original uprightness which Adam and Eve possessed before the fall. The original uprightness has been likened to innocence. Innocence merely implies absence of wrong action proceeding from ignorance of evil. That would make innocence only a negative term, but uprightness is positive. If original uprightness is no more than innocence, then babies are all born with it; but babies are *born with a positive Adamic nature.* "Behold, I was shapen in iniquity, and in sin did my mother conceive me" (Ps. 51:5). "The wicked are estranged from the womb: they go astray as soon as they be born, speaking lies" (Ps. 58:3). Original uprightness, therefore, contained a positive principle which controlled the desires and actions of nature; this was lost in the fall. Nevertheless, throughout Christ's earthly life, He was as much our Substitute under the law as when He went to the cross in our behalf. His life was as necessary to our salvation as His death; His death acquired value because it was the culmination of His life of righteousness. This righteousness is neither God's attribute nor a revealed righteousness, but a righteousness wrought by Jesus Christ in His life and death, and is manifest in salvation.

The righteousness of Christ, which was wrought out in His life and death, is revealed in the gospel (Rom. 1:16,17). What is the gospel? The gospel proclaims certain *objective facts* concerning the birth, sinless life, death, and resurrection of Christ; but these facts do not in themselves constitute the gospel. Only when these *objective facts* are associated with a *subjective deliverance* from sin is the gospel effected. The gospel, therefore, is not an offer of salvation; it is the power of God *unto salvation* (Rom. 1:16). This gospel does not come merely to inform man of objective facts; it invades man's life with a work of creation (II Cor. 5:17; Eph. 2:8-10; Ezek. 36:25-27). Faith in the recipient is not questioned. His faith, however, is not a human contribution to his salvation, but is God's gift oriented to grace. The faith of God's elect (Titus 1:1) is not something that seizes but is seized. This faith is not the power of choice, though it leads to it; it is the act which brings the will into humble submission to the righteousness of God. Only an Impeccable Saviour could work out such a righteousness for man's salvation.

The Holy Spirit applies the righteousness wrought out by Christ for the elect. "And when he is come, he will reprove the world of sin, and of righteousness, and of judgment" (John 16:8). The *sin* is not drunkenness, immorality, and dishonesty; it is *unbelief.* The Spirit convicts of *righteousness* because there is no one on earth during Christ's absence who can tell us what righteousness is. None, apart from God's grace, know what this righteousness is. The Holy Spirit must reveal God's righteousness to men.

There is a difference between John's baptism and the baptism of Christians today. The difference is between God's message to national Israel and His message to the Gentiles. John's baptism emphasized confession of the fact that they were lawbreakers. Following John, the apostles pointed to the specific sin of murdering Christ. "Ye men of Israel, hear these words; Jesus of Nazareth, a man approved of God among you by miracles and wonders and signs, which God did by him in the midst of you, as ye yourselves also know: Him, being delivered by the determinate counsel and foreknowledge of God, ye have taken, and by wicked hands have crucified and slain" (Acts 2:22,23). The deed was public; the confession must also be public. The first seven chapters of the Acts Of The Apostles are transitional. That period has long since expired. Baptism to us is not only a confession of lawbreaking and crucifying Christ, but also confession of Christ's righteousness. "And be found in him, not having mine own righteousness, which is of the law, but that which is through the faith of Christ, the righteousness which is of God by faith" (Phil. 3:9). This confession is not with a view to forgiveness, but because forgiveness has been received. "Can any man forbid water, that these should not be baptized, which have received the Holy Ghost as well as we?" (Acts 10:47). ". . . and many of the Corinthians hearing believed, and were baptized" (Acts 18:8).

Christian baptism is the answer of a good conscience toward God (I Pet. 3:20,21). It signifies that the believer has gone out of the world which is under judgment. He who is true to his baptism is like Noah in the ark; he condemns the world. The believer's conscience has been made good by the "blood of Christ" (Heb. 9:14), and this makes him fit for heaven. But to equip him to live on earth according to God's will, he needs deliverance and preservation from the power of the world. As those in the ark came *in figure* under the cover of the death of Jesus Christ, so those who are scripturally baptized come *in figure* under the cover of the death of Christ. "Know ye not, that so many of us as were baptized into Jesus Christ were baptized into his death? Therefore we are buried with him by baptism into death: that like as Christ was raised up from the dead by the glory of the Father, even so we also should walk in newness of life" (Rom. 6:3,4).

Christian baptism cannot save both really and figuratively. The Greek word for *figure* (I Pet. 3:20,21) means *a corresponding type.* This is not a case of type and antitype, but of two types. *"Saved by water"* is the type, and *"baptism"* is the corresponding type.

Noah went into the ark a saved man. He was a "just man" (Gen. 6:9), "perfect in his generation" (Gen. 6:9), "walked with God" (Gen. 6:9), "found grace in the eyes of the Lord" (Gen. 6:8), "a preacher of righteousness" (II Pet. 2:5), and "a righteous man before God" (Gen. 7:1). If baptism (the like figure) also saves us, we must possess the same qualifications as Noah. We agree that Noah was really saved; but he was really saved before he was saved by water, which was a figure of which baptism is the like figure.

There is much argument as to whether the word *figure* refers to the *ark* or to the *water.* Since the relative pronoun must agree with its antecedent in gender, the word must refer to the water. Thus, our translation reads, "which (water) also (as a) counterpart now saves you, (namely) baptism." The waters of the flood saved the inmates of the ark. Were the inmates righteous people? Yes, they were righteous and had been made so by the righteousness of God. Thus, we have baptism saving *believers* (not unbelievers); Peter says that it saves them only as a counterpart. That is, baptism is the counterpart of the reality, salvation.

Baptism is a figure and should be treated as such. As the ark was God's ordinance and not man's invention, so is baptism. As the ark was the scorn and derision of man, so is baptism. Peter said the waters of the flood saved the inmates of the ark. Thus, the flood waters buoyed up the ark above their death-dealing powers and saved those inside the ark. The very waters that were death to the rest of the human race were life to all who were in the ark. The former were drowned because they were not rightly related to the waters (the Judgment of God). Those who were saved were rightly related to the righteousness of God, and could say, "There is therefore no condemnation (Judgment) to them which are in Christ Jesus" (Rom. 8:1).

There has never been but one way of salvation, and that way is grace. It is not grace plus works that saves, but grace alone produces salvation. "And if by grace, then is it no more of works: otherwise grace is no more grace . . ." (Rom. 11:6). It is not Jesus Christ (Matt. 1:21) plus baptism that saves, but Christ alone is Saviour (Luke 19:10). The Old and New Testament saints are saved by the same grace. Moses and the prophets preached the same message as the means of salvation that Paul preached. Paul, who was sent to the Gentiles with the message of deliverance, preached *"none other things"* than those which Moses and the prophets proclaimed: "That Christ should suffer, and that he should be the first that should rise from the dead, and should shew light unto the people, and to the Gentiles" (Acts 26:22,23). As Moses said nothing about baptism, so Paul did not associate baptism with Christ for salvation as so many claim.

CHRIST'S TEMPTATION

The Lord Jesus ascended from the baptismal water to go into solitude against Satan. As the *Beloved Son* He came forth from baptism; as the *Son of Man* He came forth from temptation. The Jordan lies on the heavenly side, and the wilderness on the earthly side of the Saviour. He, therefore, stepped out of the water of baptism into the fire of temptation. "And immediately the Spirit driveth him into the wilderness. And he was there in the wilderness forty days, tempted of Satan; and was with the wild beasts; and the angels ministered unto him" (Mark 1:12,13). "For we have not an high priest which cannot be touched with the feeling of our infirmities; but was in all points tempted like as we are, yet without sin" (Heb. 4:15).

The temptation was an actual meeting between a personal Saviour and a personal Devil. Satan, not our Lord, was put to the test in the wilderness. He was unmasked, but our Lord was revealed in the perfection of His Manhood. Adam, a man God created, is viewed in the garden of Eden; here we see Jesus Christ, the God-Man begotten by the Holy Spirit by eternal generation. The Devil challenged the first man; the second Man challenged the Devil. Satan ruined the first man; the second Man ". . . spoiled principalities and powers, he made a shew of them openly, triumphing over them in it" (Col. 2:15). He beat the Devil as the God-Man, the Man in a position of weakness.

Mark uses the strongest language of any Evangelist; he said the Saviour was *driven* into the wilderness. We must be careful not to misapply this strong expression to mean that our Lord went into the wilderness against His own will. The word *driveth* means *to thrust forth* with the suggestion of force; hence, to drive out by force. *The driving force came from within Himself.* His own mind and heart worked together to drive Him from the presence of men to meet Satan alone. When Scripture states that He was "driven by the Spirit," it means that His mind and heart were so full of the Holy Spirit that He, not the Devil, must be the driving force.

Were Christ's temptations, sufferings, and death wrought in appearance only? Those who believe in peccability say, "If Jesus could not yield to temptation, then his temptations were not real. He only pretended to be tempted when he really was not. This would make him guilty of hypocrisy which is condemned more than any other sin." The contest our Lord had with Satan was a reality. It was not a sham battle. Satan's attack against our Lord began in Eden, the garden of God (Ezek. 28:13). He was present in the Adamic Eden as an apostate spirit and tempter (Gen. 3); but in Eden, the garden of God, his rebellion began as a minister of God. His assault against Christ was continued in the days of Christ's earthly sojourn.

Nowhere in the Old Testament is it said that God was tempted by Satan, nor is it said in the gospel of John that Jesus Christ was tempted. The incarnation made *the reality of Christ's temptation* possible. John presents Him as God; God absolutely considered cannot be tempted. James said, "Let no man say when he is tempted, I am tempted of God: for *God cannot be tempted with evil,* neither tempteth he any man" (James 1:13). The incarnate Christ was tempted, but *the idea that temptability implies susceptibility is heresy.* For example, the temptation of a drunken party would have little chance of causing one who is Spirit-filled to fall; nevertheless, a person addicted to drink would be easily led astray. The temptation might be the same in both cases, but the ones tempted would have contrasting powers of resistance. This is the reason James said, "But every man is tempted when he is drawn away of his *own lust* and *enticed*" (James 1:14). Man converts testing into temptation; *own lust* is connected with man's inward weakness, and *enticed* points to the outward attraction. Man blames his circumstances, but circumstances are nothing more than providence. Providence provides only the *objects;* the *cause* is man's depraved heart.

Would anyone be so ungodly as to suggest that Jesus Christ had an internal weakness that could manifest itself in the lusts of the flesh? There is wicked folly in every unsaved person, and that folly makes him measure God by the creature. His wicked logic is that since he can be tempted, so God can be tempted. Such evil logic is for the purpose of furthering unclean intents; the whore has her vows and peace offerings to further her wantonness. Solomon said, "That they may keep thee from the strange woman, from the stranger which flattereth with her words. For at the window of my house I looked through my casement, And beheld among the simple ones, I discerned among the youths, a young man void of understanding, Passing through the street near her corner; and he went the way to her house. In the twilight, in the evening, in the black and dark night: And, behold, there met him a woman with the attire of an harlot, and subtil of heart. (She is loud and stubborn; her feet abide not in her house: Now is she without, now in the streets, and lieth in wait at every corner.) So she caught him, and kissed him, and with an impudent face said unto him, *I have peace offerings with me; this day have I payed my vows*" (Prov. 7:5-14). The religionist who says that Jesus Christ "could have sinned" is using the language of a harlot.

Temptation has three meanings: (1) *A trial of faith* for the purpose of bringing out some hidden virtue or to prove a person (James 1:2; I Pet. 1:6; John 6:6; Heb. 11:17); (2) *A solicitation to do wrong* (James 1:14; I Tim. 6:9; Luke 4:13); and (3) *A trying or challenging of God by men* (Ps. 95:9; 106:14; I Cor. 10:9).

God tests for man's good, desiring only his blessing; the Devil tests with an evil motive, desiring only man's ruin. It has been objected that if Christ could not have yielded to temptation, then His temptation was an act of hypocrisy. This objection is merely superficial. *His temptation proved His character not to Himself, but to the world.* Christ's character was proved to be absolutely holy. The testing, however, in no way indicates that the conflict between Christ and Satan was not real. For example, the testing of tires by dropping an automobile from twenty feet in the air in no way indicates that the impact between the tires and the ground was not real. The test is to prove not that they can blow out but that they cannot blow out. The temptation of Christ was not to prove He had the capacity to sin, but that He could not sin. When you test wood with fire, you have ashes; water with fire, evaporation; steel with fire, dust; gold with fire, dross; but Jesus Christ had no Adamic dross to be consumed. The first Adam was tempted from *within;* the Second from *without.* There was no weakness in Christ to be attracted to allurement without.

The incarnate Son of God was tempted, but *there was not the inner struggle of the two natures* as in the case of Paul (Rom. 7). Both natures of Christ were holy. It is true that He was tempted in all points like as we are *except on the question of sin* (Heb. 4:15). If *"tempted in all points"* means what those who embrace peccability say it does, then their theory must be carried to its logical conclusion. Here is a whoremonger that is saved, but in a moment of weakness he looks upon a woman to lust after her. He knows ". . . That whosoever looketh on a woman to lust after her hath committed adultery with her already in his heart" (Matt. 5:28). He is convicted of his sin and falls on his face before his High Priest. His reasoning is, according to the theory of peccability, since Christ was touched with the feeling of his infirmities he understands his problem. He would say, as it were, "You understand my problem, for you too were tempted in all points like me. You did not yield, but you were tempted; therefore, you know how to sympathize with me in my problem." All who hold to this heresy think that God is altogether like themselves (Ps. 50:21). *They have a human god and know not the God of the Bible.*

Luke presents the perfect humanity of Christ. He gives the order of the three temptations with reference to body, soul, and spirit—the three spheres of manhood. In each sphere we have the attraction of the world, the flesh, and the Devil. As to the world, Christ said, "I am not of this world" (John 17:16); the world has no claim on Him. As to His flesh, He did not have the fallen Adamic nature; therefore, His saving work could extend to the *nature of sin* as well as to the *sins of nature.* "For such an high priest became us, who is holy, harmless, undefiled, separate from sinners, and made higher than the heavens" (Heb. 7:26). If He had a fallen nature, then he could not save himself nor anyone else. As to the Devil, He said, "the prince of this world cometh and hath nothing in Me" (John 14:30). The words, "Hath nothing in Me," mean that Satan shall find nothing wrong in Christ. He had no sin; this can be said of none but the Lord. Satan, however, tried to persuade Christ to act independently of God. Our Lord's earthly mission was one of obedience to the will of the Father, and Satan's offer held no attraction for Him.

In our Lord's first temptation, He refused to exercise power to provide bread because there was no word to do so (Deut. 8:3). This proves we are not to do anything for which we have no Scripture. This destroys all traditions. Man must live more by that which comes out of the mouth of God than by earthly food which goes into his own mouth. With the Christian all that is not prescribed in the Word of God is forbidden. This was a time of political oppression and unemployment. The parable of the laborers is a commentary on the economic condition of Christ's day (Matt. 20). *Satan attacked Christ's virtue* (compassion) because *our Lord had no vice.* The temptation was to eat bread without sweat, and this is contrary to Scripture (Gen. 3:19; II Thess. 3:10). Here is a demonstration of *socialism* because socialism is concerned with the temporal desires of man.

In the second temptation holiness refused to give honor to Satan which was due only to God. *The Holy One must receive Kingship from none but God* Who promised it (Luke 19:12-15). On earth we see the glory of world kingdoms; this was the glory Satan offered Christ. This glory of world kingdoms resides in Satan's power since Adam surrendered his dominion to him through the fall. The Father had another plan for His Son before He would receive the glory of God's Kingdom. Through that plan the Father would give the heathen for the Son's inheritance. The glory of this world speaks of *materialism;* this is the spirit that characterizes the Laodician age (Rev. 3:14-20). Such glory our Lord refused from Satan.

The third temptation manifests Holiness refusing to try God's faithfulness. The Lord Jesus would not place God in a position where He would be forced to aid Him. He was not to dazzle people with some sensational act, for sensationalism is contrary to the will of God. The person who is dwelling in God's love does not need any sign or miracle to make him sure of God's love and care. One living in the knowledge of love has no desire to put that love to the test; to do so would prove distrust. Thus, we see Christ's perfect trust in the Father.

There is no evil in temptation itself. Men are tempted to outward sin by indwelling sin. Paul said, "For I know that in me (that is, in my flesh,) dwelleth no good thing . . ." (Rom. 7:18). Jesus Christ had no *indwelling sin;* therefore, He was never tempted to *outward sin.* This in no way refutes the reality of the contest but proves that He was not tempted (tried) in the same way men are tempted (allured).

In each temptation Jesus Christ relied on the Word of God to defeat Satan. Every avenue of attack had been tried and failed. There was nothing else Satan could do. Satan had exhausted himself. He departed for a little season but soon prevailed to bruise the heel of Christ; our Lord, however, bruised his head. "Forasmuch then as the children are partakers of flesh and blood, he also likewise took part of the same; that through death he might destroy him that had the power of death, that is, the devil" (Heb. 2:14). Our Saviour, therefore, has left us only a vanquished enemy to contend with in this world.

CHRIST'S IMPECCABLE LIFE

The Lord Jesus Christ was God's representative Man. There was never anything needed to commend Him but Himself, for He was the Impeccable Christ. "For such an high priest became us, who is holy, harmless, undefiled, separate from sinners, and made higher than the heavens" (Heb. 7:26). Jesus Christ was not an unclean Jew who needed an offering for his own sin, but He was the spotless sacrifice to be offered for sin. He touched the leper, but He was not defiled. Christ had God's relationship to sin because He was God. He would have been defiled if He had been clothed in a peccable nature. The Saviour was not merely undefiled; *He was undefilable.* As God's representative Man, He was undefilable in every aspect of His earthly life. Thus, when His earthly **sojourn** was completed, He went *straightway* to God as the "sheaf of the firstfruits" (Lev. 23:10).

The sheaf was taken, *just as it was,* out of the field (field is a type of the world) ; it needed no process to prepare it for the presence and acceptance of God. This proves that Christ was not peccable while He was on earth; if He were peccable on earth, then He could not have been taken *as He was* and presented to God. Every descendant of Adam would be without hope if Christ had been peccable; nevertheless, there is hope because His Impeccable life qualified Him to be the Impeccable Sacrifice for sin.

The meat offering typifies Christ in His perfect life (Lev. 2). This offering was *bloodless;* it presents all the symbols of the holy character of our Lord Jesus Christ in His earthly life. Such features of character could never be found anywhere but in Christ. Our Saviour in His incarnation retained that self-affirming purity which is holiness. The life He lived was a practical demonstration of that holiness. What other living person could have faced his enemies and challenged them with these words, "Which of you convinceth me of sin?" (John 8:46). The *inherent purity of Christ* was so perfect that not even perjured witnesses could prove, to the satisfaction of a prejudiced court, one charge against His holiness. This means that people who see Christ as a peccable person are worse than the perjured witnesses and the prejudiced court of our Lord's trial.

The meat offering is found constantly in conjunction with *burnt* and *peace offerings*, but never with *sin* or *trespass offerings*. He must live *as Man* before He could die *for men*. The meat offering reveals the perfect character of the sinless and holy God-Man. "For such an high priest became us, who is holy, harmless, undefiled, separate from sinners, and made higher than the heavens" (Heb. 7:26).

Fine flour was the basis of the offering. It was free from every unevenness, coarseness, or spot; otherwise, it could never typify the Lord Jesus Who was "a lamb without blemish and without spot" (I Pet. 1:19). Men could not improve the Light Who was shining; they could only be melted or hardened by Him. No attempt was made to trim or order this Light, for neither the tongs nor the snuffdishes were needed. They had no connection with Christ; consequently, those who sought to challenge or rebuke Him went away rebuked and put to shame. He never had to recall a word or retrace a step throughout His Impeccable Life. God's delight in Him was ever expressing itself; the Lord Jesus said, "And he that sent me is with me: the Father hath not left me alone; for I do always those things that please him" (John 8:29). There was no unevenness in any of His graces.

Oil is typical of the Holy Spirit and may be applied in a twofold way: (1) *mingled*—in the miraculous conception of the human nature in the womb of Mary; and (2) *poured*—in the anointing of Christ, for He was given the Spirit without measure. The Holy Spirit could never have come into contact with every grain of that "fine flour" if there had been any peccability in it. There is nothing but Impeccability, to the most minute detail, in Christ's life. The Holy Humanity and Impeccable Life of Christ are to be sacredly guarded by His saints in the face of the infidelity which is abounding. These truths are as essential to Christianity as His Deity.

Frankincense speaks of everything Christ did in life going up as a sweet savour unto God (John 4:34; 19:30). The name of the Lord Jesus Christ is as "ointment poured forth" (S. of S. 1:3). His *name* is Himself. It is the expression of all that He *is*: His lowliness, grace, excellency, purity, power, and perfection. *We must, therefore, be attracted to the Lord Jesus because of Who He is, not* merely for what He does. Eve was attracted to the tree in the garden of Eden because of what she wanted from it. The result was spiritual, moral, and physical disaster. As Christians we "sit down under His shadow" and find the Impeccable Saviour to be all that we need. ". . . I sat down under his shadow with great delight, and his fruit was sweet to my taste" (S. of S. 2:3).

The meat offering was to be made *without leaven*. Leaven argues corruption in doctrine (Matt. 16:6,11,12), morals (I Cor. 5:6-8), and hypocrisy (Luke 12:1,2). Leaven, therefore, could have no place in the Person and work of the Impeccable Saviour. Scripture states: (1) *He knew no sin* (II Cor. 5:21). The word *knew* does not refer to the prescience of God, for in this sense He knew all things; it means to know in an intimate way (to become associated with) as Adam knew Eve (Gen. 4:1). (2) *In Him was no sin* (Heb. 7:26). (3) *He did no sin* (John 8:46). He could not be convicted of sin because in Him was "no sin."

Honey, as well as leaven, *was excluded from the offering.* Honey was a symbol of natural sweetness. The meat offering had no honey in it (Lev. 2: 11), nor did Jesus Christ have any honey in His Impeccable life because He was the true meat offering. The will of God is ever the rule of His life. He could never be drawn into softness by nature's sweetness. He knew how to give nature and its relationships their proper place. Peter used a bit of *nature's honey* when he said, in answer to Christ's statement concerning His suffering, "Be it far from thee" (Matt. 16:22). This honey soured as soon as it fell from the lips of Peter; for Christ answered, ". . . Get thee behind me, Satan: thou art an offense unto me: for thou savourest not the things that be of God, but those that be of men (the sweetness of human nature)" (Matt. 16:23).

Every offering of the meat offering was to be seasoned with *salt*. "And every oblation of thy meat offering shalt thou season with *salt;* neither shalt thou suffer *the salt of the covenant* of thy God to be lacking from thy meat offering: with all thine offerings thou shalt offer salt" (Lev. 2:13). "The salt of the covenant of thy God" is an expression which attracts the attention of every Christian. A close observation of Leviticus shows that other things were needed in connection with the sacrifices offered by the Israelites. *Their sacrifices were imperfect;* therefore, *frankincense, oil,* and *salt* were needed to make them acceptable to God. God did not smell sweet savour in the sacrifices unless *frankincense* was added. This means that the best performances of Christians are not acceptable to God without the merit of Christ constraining them (II Cor. 5:14). The Israelites were required to use *oil* in their offerings because it was a type of the Holy Spirit. What is prayer or the sacrifice of praise without the Holy Spirit to give them life? That which goes to God must first come from God (Rom. 8:26,27). And *salt,* which is the principal of faithfulness, excludes the activities of the flesh because it is the preservative power of fidelity. The salt penetrates the sacrifice and drives away corruption. We come infinitely short of what we behold by faith in the Person of our Saviour, but the salt is a symbol of the purpose of heart to pursue conformity to Him. The Christian therefore is the *salt of the earth,* and *his speech is to be seasoned with salt* (Matt. 5:13; Col. 4:6).

The salt of the covenant speaks of the unchangeable and incorruptible covenant of God. When God made a covenant with David, it is written, "Ought ye not to know that the Lord God of Israel gave the kingdom over Israel to David for ever, even to him and to his sons *by a covenant of salt?*" (II Chron. 13:5). The "everlasting covenant" (Heb. 13:20,21) is the only ladder reaching from heaven to earth. The blessings of this covenant come to us through obligations fulfilled in Jesus Christ for us. If anything can make man praise God, it is his knowledge of the covenant and that he is in it. God deserves exclusive glory, and covenant theology is the only theology that glorifies God. Nothing constrains the Christian to such activity and zeal in the cause of Christ as a sense of covenant love.

The sheaf is set forth in the feast of first-fruits as a type of Divine promise and purpose. This type was fulfilled in Christ's resurrection. He had perfectly glorified the Father during His earthly life, and now His Impeccable Life had ripened into fruition. The Lord Jesus Christ said, ". . . Now is the Son of man glorified, and God is glorified in him. If God be glorified in him, God shall also glorify him in himself, and shall straightway glorify him" (John 13:31,32). This is Christ's recognition of His title to personal glory. As He had perfectly glorified the Father on earth, so it was but a natural thing that *He should enter heaven on His own personal glory.* His Impeccable *moral glory* must be fully displayed before His Impeccable *royal glory* can be manifested. The opened heaven at the beginning of Christ's ministry manifested the full acceptance of *His Impeccable Person;* the opened heaven at the end of His ministry revealed the full acceptance of *His Impeccable work.*

Jesus Christ personally stood on earth in our nature; not for Himself, but as a pledge and earnest of all the harvest. This first sheaf is the pledge of both our resurrection and acceptance. "But every man in his own order: Christ the firstfruits; afterward they that are Christ's at his coming. Then cometh the end, when he shall have delivered up the kingdom to God, even the Father; when he shall have put down all rule and all authority and power. For he must reign, till he hath put all enemies under his feet" (I Cor. 15:23-25).

The sheaf of the harvest was a *single sheaf.* It was taken directly from the field and waved—*as it was*—before the Lord. Jesus Christ, our Impeccable Saviour and Representative, was taken from the world and waved—*as He was*—before the Lord as the Firstfruits of the resurrection. The single sheaf represents the Lord Jesus Christ in many respects: (1) *One* with the Father in nature and essence (John 10:30); (2) *One* in His Person though He possesses both the Divine and human natures (John 1:1,14; Phil. 2:5-8); (3) *One* with reference to the sacrifice for sin (Heb. 10:10,14); (4) *One* in His office as Mediator (I Tim. 2:5); (5) *One* with respect of hope (Eph. 4:4; Titus 2:11-14); (6) *One* with regard to Headship (I Cor. 11:3; Col. 1:18); and (7) *One* with reference to Lordship (Eph. 4:5; Rev. 19:16).

THE GOD APPROVED MAN

The Impeccable Saviour is the Man Whom God approved. "Ye men of Israel, hear these words; Jesus of Nazareth, a man approved of God among you by miracles and wonders and signs, which God did by him in the midst of you, as ye yourselves also know" (Acts 2:22). Lost men have no faith in this God approved Man. Before His departure from the disciples the Saviour said, "... It is expedient for you that I go away: for if I go not away, the Comforter will not come unto you; but if I depart, I will send him unto you. And when he is come, he will reprove the world of sin, and of righteousness, and of judgment: Of sin, because *they believe not on me*" (John 16:7-9). Since *man* sinned, justice required that *man must give the satisfaction.* "Wherefore, as by one *man* sin entered into the world, and death by sin; and so death passed upon all men, for that all have sinned" (Rom. 5:12). Justice has been satisfied in the "man approved of God." "Be it known unto you therefore, men and brethren, that through *this man* is preached unto you the forgiveness of sins: And *by him all that believe are justified from all things,* from which ye could not be justified by the law of Moses" (Acts 13:38,39).

Jesus Christ is *more than man;* He is the God-Man. The fact that Christ is Mediator and Saviour as God-Man shows the serious heresy of those who deny that He is the Impeccable Man as well as God. The *flesh* of the God-Man is perfect. Paul warned the Christians at Philippi about putting confidence in the flesh. "For we are the circumcision, which worship God in the spirit, and rejoice in Christ Jesus, and have no confidence in the flesh" (Phil. 3:3). The Christian, however, does have *confidence in the flesh of the man approved of God* because He is God manifest in Impeccable Flesh. Christians rejoice in the *flesh* and *blood* of the Man Christ Jesus, knowing that His flesh is meat indeed and His blood is drink indeed (John 6:55). Such Divine joy is the result of the perfect Man Who is Lord and Saviour.

The Lord Jesus Christ is *objectively* presented to the saints as *"the God approved Man,"* but He dwells *subjectively* in them by the Holy Spirit, and this Spirit is called "the Spirit of Christ" (Rom. 8:9). There are two serious errors concerning the Son of God, namely: (1) Many are looking only on what Jesus Christ has done and suffered objectively on the cross. They rest on a faith that is historical or traditional without looking for a subjective witness by the Holy Spirit. "He that believeth on the Son of God *hath the witness in himself*" (I John 5:10). "The Spirit itself beareth witness *with our spirit*, that we are the children of God" (Rom. 8:16). The Holy Spirit alone can cause the light of salvation to shine in the dark heart (II Cor. 4:6). (2) There are others who contend for what they call a subjective experience of grace, but they are opposed to the objective Christ Who was Impeccable. A peccable Christ within is not salvation. What is true salvation? Salvation is the regenerating Holy Spirit working within a person and leading that one outside of himself to the Impeccable Saviour as the object of true faith.

Jesus Christ came in the *fulness of time* (Gal. 4:4). "But when the fulness of the time was come, God sent forth his Son made of a woman ... " All the purposes of God run on schedule. The time had reached its fulness for the incarnation because it was the time ordained by God. The word *fulness* proves that time has a fulness; this time comes by degrees. There is a time when time is not full. Christ said, "Go ye up unto this feast: I go not up yet unto this feast; for *my time is not yet full come*" (John 7:8). On the other hand, there is a time when time reaches its fulness. The Saviour said, ". . . The hour is come, that the Son of man should be glorified" (John 12:23). *Time has now reached its fulness.* He, in Whom the *fulness* of the Godhead dwells bodily (Col. 2:9), in Whom the *fulness* of grace and truth are found (John 1:14), Whom God sent forth in the *fulness* of time, came in order that the elect might of His fulness receive, and grace for grace (John 1:16).

God *sent forth* His Son (Gal. 4:4). If we desire to know the excellency of the Sender, we must consider the excellency of the Person sent. There is no greater than His only begotten Son. "For in him dwelleth all the fulness of the Godhead bodily" (Col. 2:9). The sending forth of His Son to be made of a woman is to be distinguished from the *theophanies* of the Old Testament. Theophanies were temporary pre-incarnate manifestations of Jesus Christ, but the sending forth of His Son to be made of a woman would be permanent. This permanency was in order that God might dwell with His redeemed forever (Ex. 25:8; John 1:14; Rev. 21:3). The statement, "sent forth," demands study. It refers to the act of one who sends another with a commission to do something, and the person sent is given credentials to perform his commission. Nowhere is it indicated that the Father sent forth the Son and then anxiously awaited the Son's reaction to the work He was sent to accomplish. God came from the eternal shore to rescue sinking sinners.

God sent forth His Son *made of a woman* (Gal. 4:4). This was the manner of His coming. *How can He Who is Maker be sent made?* "*All* things were *made* by him; and without him was not any thing *made* that was *made*" (John 1:3). The Son "sent forth" into the world is one thing, and His being "made of a woman" is another. The first proves His Deity; the second confirms His humanity. He was not created like Adam nor begotten by man as man, but He was "made of a woman" which is sometimes translated "born of a woman." The word was carefully chosen to express the power of God in His mysterious incarnation.

Jesus Christ was *made under the law*. The three parts of the law are moral, civil, and ceremonial. (1) *The God approved Man was subject to the moral law*. Every man is subject to God and His law. Solomon said, "Let us hear the conclusion of the whole matter: Fear God, and keep his commandments: for this is the whole duty of man" (Eccl. 12:13). Christ was made under the moral law as the *surety* of His people, and He declared His willingness to fulfill this obligation by saying, "Lo, I come . . . to do thy will, O my God! Yea, thy law is within my heart" (Ps. 40:7,8). A surety is a person who agrees to be responsible for the debt of another. Judah said to Joseph, " For thy servant became surety for the lad unto my father . . ." (Gen. 44:32). The surety, therefore, is to pay the debt of the original owner. Judah was a type of the Lord Jesus Who became the surety of His people. "For as by one man's disobedience many were made sinners, so by the *obedience of one* shall many be made righteous" (Rom. 5:19). "By so much was Jesus made a surety of a better testament" (Heb. 7:22). (2) *The God approved Man was subject to the civil law*. Christ was by birth a Jew (John 4:22; Heb. 7:14; Rev. 5:5) ; therefore, it was proper that He should be subject to their civil government. He taught subjection to the civil law, but His enemies falsely charged Him with sedition (Matt. 17:24-27; 22:17-21). (3) *Christ was subject to the ceremonial law*. "And when eight days were accomplished for the circumcising of the child, his name was called Jesus, which was so named of the angel before he was conceived in the womb" (Luke 2:21). Every person that was circumcised became a debtor to the whole law (Gal. 5:3). Christ's circumcision was an earnest that He would, when the time came, shed all His blood. The debt of a capital law is death. Therefore, He must shed all His blood for the satisfaction of a capital law. His name of "Saviour" was publicly proclaimed at His circumcision (shedding of blood was a pledge).

Jesus Christ *was crucified* by wicked hands. The Son of the virgin was *a Man approved by miracles and wonders and signs;* nevertheless, He was delivered by the determinate counsel and foreknowledge of God and put to death by wicked hands (Acts 2:22,23). The intense hatred of wicked men does not prevent the fulfillment of God's purpose. "But *this man,* after he had offered one sacrifice for sins for ever, sat down on the right hand of God" (Heb. 10:12). The Son born of the virgin was Man; but Man absolutely considered could never satisfy justice, forgive sins, or obtain eternal redemption. Therefore, Jesus Christ was "the true God and eternal life" (I John 5:20).

Jesus Christ *ascended to the right hand of the Father.* "But now is Christ risen from the dead, and become the firstfruits of them that slept. For since by man came death, *by man came also the resurrection of the dead"* (I Cor. 15:20,21). Christ Who *descended* is the same Who *ascended;* He descended *without a body* but ascended *with a body.* The eternal Son came into the womb of Mary without a body, but He came out of the womb with a body. In that same body he "... ascended up far above all heavens, that He might fill all things" (Eph. 4:10).

Two men stood by in white apparel when our Lord ascended saying, "... Ye men of Galilee, why stand ye gazing up into heaven? this *same Jesus,* which is taken up from you into heaven, shall so come in like manner as ye have seen him go into heaven" (Acts 1:11). They looked *objectively,* not *subjectively,* as the Son of Man ascended. The Saviour ascending was the Son of *Man* with flesh and bones. "Behold my hands and my feet, that it is I myself; handle me, and see; for a spirit hath not flesh and bones, as ye see me have" (Luke 24:39). Christ as God absolutely considered could not ascend because He is omnipresent. He came from heaven by

His incarnation and remained in heaven by Deity; He descended to the earth but did not leave heaven. Christ as the God approved Man did ascend to heaven (Eph. 4:8-10). His *body* which was prepared for Him ascended to a place where it was not before. *Christ's body, though glorified, is not Deified.* It is not infinite; therefore, it cannot be in heaven and on earth at the same time. This refutes the doctrine of transubstantiation.

Jesus Christ is making *intercession in heaven for saints on earth.* "For Christ is not entered into the holy places made with hands, which are the figures of the true; but into heaven itself, now to appear in the presence of God for us" (Heb. 9:24). "For every high priest is ordained to offer gifts and sacrifices; wherefore it is of necessity that *this man* have somewhat also to offer" (Heb. 8:3). It is for men that *the God approved Man* became a High Priest. Our Saviour is Mediator of a better covenant which was established upon better promises. A mediator is a person who stands between two parties and represents each party to the other party. Jesus Christ is Mediator between God and man; He is the Daysman Who lays His hands on both. He reconciles man to God by the blood of His cross and appears in the presence of God to intercede for all whom he reconciles (Heb. 7:24,25).

Jesus Christ is *coming for the saints.* When He comes the second time, He will descend from the place where He is now as the ascended Lord and Saviour. The meeting of Christ and His saints will be in the air; therefore, Christ descends to meet the saints, and the saints ascend to meet their Lord. "For the Lord himself shall descend from heaven with a shout, with the voice of the archangel, and with the trump of God: and the dead in Christ shall rise first: Then we which are alive and remain shall be caught up together with them in the clouds, to meet the Lord in the air: and so shall we ever be with the Lord" (I Thess. 4:16,17).

The *God approved Man* ascended, after He finished His work, to heaven in order that He might send the Holy Spirit to reveal Himself to the hearts of men. Now we have the *subjective Spirit* focusing our attention on the *objective* fact of *Jesus Christ as the Man approved of God.*

CHRIST'S PRAYER LIFE

The fact of Impeccability is proved by Christ's unique prayer life. *Our Lord never accepted the fellowship of men in prayer* because there was an essential difference in nature. Had His human nature been peccable, He could have fellowshipped His disciples in prayer. However, when He invited the disciples to watch with Him, He enjoined them to pray for *themselves.* Our Lord never requested the prayers of men for Himself. No man ever prayed *for Him;* no man ever prayed *with Him.* Thus, the Saviour in His unique prayer life not only revealed His Deity but also His Impeccable human nature. *"Who in the days of his flesh,* when he had *offered up prayers* and supplications with strong crying and tears unto him that was able to save him from death, and was heard in that he feared; Though he were a Son, yet learned he obedience by the things which he suffered; And being made perfect, he became the author of eternal salvation unto all them that obey him; Called of God an high priest after the order of Melchisedec" (Heb. 5:7-10).

Christ did not pray in the capacity of the eternal Son of God, but in the position as Mediator. As God absolutely considered He had no one to whom He could pray for either help or comfort. Deity could not receive from anyone; He was dependent on none. Deity assumed a human nature, and the Son of God became the Son of Man; therefore, as the God-Man He prayed.

The only recorded prayer of Jesus Christ is found in John 17. Matthew 6:9-15 is commonly called the Lord's prayer, but the Impeccable Saviour could never have said, "forgive *us* our sins" (Luke 11:4). Christ's Impeccability is denied when one associates Him with the model prayer (Matt. 6:9-15). The brief but comprehensive prayer of Christ for His own is recorded in John 17. In this prayer Christ prayed to the Father for the glory of God to be manifested.

The Lord Jesus prayed in the days of His flesh. This was true because He was Man. We should be horrified at any person who diminishes the glory of the Godhead, but we should also be appalled if anyone takes from Christ the truth of His humanity. To deny His humanity destroys His sacrificial death and glorious resurrection. Thus, we would have no gospel, and if no gospel, no hope. The term, *"the days of his flesh,"* is used to distinguish His life on earth from His former state in glory. Eternity is not the day of His flesh.

The Saviour, during the days of His flesh, prayed *"unto him that was able to save him from death"* (Heb. 5:7). This Scripture is generally interpreted to mean that Christ prayed to be saved from death. The passage, however, does not say that He prayed to be saved from death; but He prayed "unto *him that was able* to save him from death." The Father could have saved His Son *from death* had it been His will, but His eternal purpose was to save Him *through death* (Heb. 2:14). Luke records Christ's prayer of submission to His Father's will. "And he was withdrawn from them about a stone's cast, and kneeled down, and prayed, Saying, Father, if thou be willing, remove this cup from me: nevertheless not my will, but thine, be done" (Luke 22:41,42).

Christ's prayer was "heard in that *he feared.*" The Greek word for fear in this passage is *eulabeia*, which means that mingled fear and love, combined, constitute true piety (reverence) of man toward God. Other Greek words translated *fear* are (1) *phobos*, which means flight caused by being scared (Acts 2:43; I Cor. 2:3; I Tim. 5:20; Heb. 2:15; I John 4:18); (2) *deilia*, a fearfulness not given to the children of God (II Tim. 1:7); (3) *deilos*, a person who is either cowardly or timid (Matt. 8:26; Mark 4:40); and (4) *entromos*, a person who trembles with fear (Acts 7:32; 16:29). These last four Greek words for fear could never refer to the One about Whom it was said, "The Lord God hath opened mine ear, and I *was not rebellious, neither turned away back. I gave my back to the smiters, and my cheeks to them that plucked off the hair: I hid not my face from shame and spitting"* (Is. 50:5,6). The Son, Who was in perfect submission to the will of the Father (Ps. 40:7,8; Heb. 10:7), viewed the Father as able to preserve Him in death from the power of death. Therefore, He must triumph on the cross and rise out from among the dead in resurrection power.

Christ's death was for the penalty of sin. The death of the Christian is not a penalty for sin; that was paid in the death of Christ. Our Saviour saw before Him, in the days of His flesh, all the pain of the cross both mental and physical. Death, however, had no personal or direct relation to Christ; He had no death in Himself. At no time was the Son of God in danger of death. Death is the result of sin; where there is no sin, death has no claim. The Son of God could never die under any attack by the enemy. "Thinkest thou that I cannot now pray to my Father, and he shall presently give me more than twelve legions of angels?" (Matt. 26:53).

The humanity of Christ appears in His prayer, for God absolutely considered cannot pray. He felt the awfulness of His anticipated sufferings and was completely resigned to those sufferings. His offering, therefore, was a free will sacrifice. His perfect reverence for the Father enabled Him to say, ". . . The cup which my Father hath given me, shall I not drink it?" (John 18:11). There was always perfect resignation to the will of God which was eternally known to Him. Purely human feelings would be unwilling to drink the cup; but the human nature of Christ, motivated by the Divine nature, made the Person of Christ willing. The Divine Person saw the will of God fall into that bitter cup, and this is what made the contents of the cup bearable. " . . . who for the joy that was set before him endured the cross . . . " (Heb. 12:2). The "strong cryings and tears" were caused by Christ's knowledge of the imputation of man's guilt to Himself from the hand of God; not from the hands of men.

How can the fear of the Impeccable Christ be reconciled with " . . . perfect love casteth out fear . . . "? (I John 4:18). Was the love of Jesus Christ imperfect? The love between the Father and Son was *absolutely perfect* during the days of Christ's flesh. A cloud, however, came between Jesus Christ and His Father. Divine justice demanded, in the interest of Divine law, the execution of the penal sentence. His offering for sin must be perfected; Divine justice must have accomplished its perfect work before the love of God could be made perfect to sinners. Thus the statement, "perfect love casteth out fear," refers to the *recipients of that perfect love;* whereas, the statement, "was heard in that he feared," refers to the *Perfector of the perfected love.*

The perfecting of saints in love depends on our being as Christ *is* "in this world" (I John 4:17). Christians are in the world, not as Christ *was when He was in it* but *as He is now.* The agonies of Calvary and the satisfaction of justice are now behind Christ. He lives no more in anticipation of judgment on sin because He has offered Himself as a sacrifice for sin (Heb. 10:10-14). The children of God may now have boldness in the day of judgment because *as he is* (with reference to perfected love through satisfied justice), so are we in this world (our love is perfected through judgment on sin and satisfied justice). The recipients of "perfected love" are free from condemnation. "There is therefore now no condemnation to them which are in Christ Jesus ... " (Rom. 8:1).

THE DRAWING POWER OF CHRIST

The Cross is the center of Christ's drawing power. "And I, if I be lifted up from the earth, will draw all men unto me" (John 12:32). Our Lord's character, though spotless white, does not draw men to salvation. This takes nothing from the blessed Person of Christ because His Impeccable nature gave merit to the sacrifice. The drawing power of God to salvation is the sacrifice of the Impeccable Person, Jesus Christ the Lord. The special influence of the Cross is the power that draws men to God for reconciliation. Man's depraved nature is drawn *by sin* from God; he must be drawn by *grace* from sin to God. Many believe that the life of Christ provides enough attraction to save a person, but such is not the truth of the gospel. The sinner can find peace only in the peace that was made through the blood of Christ's Cross (Col. 1:20).

The extent of drawing is found in the words "all men" (John 12:32). The meaning of *universal terms* must be determined by the context. The words of our text were spoken to the Greeks who said, "Sir, we would see Jesus" (John 12:21). The benefits of Christ's redemption were not restricted to the elect Jews. There were other sheep which were not of the fold of Judaism. "And *other sheep I have,* which are not of this fold; them also I must bring, and they shall hear my voice; and there shall be one fold, and one shepherd" (John 10:16). The Greeks, as well as the Jews, were included in the redemptive work of Christ. "And not for that nation only, but that also he should gather together in one the children of God that were scattered abroad" (John 11:52). *All men* could never mean all persons without exception because there were many then, as now, who had no will to come to Christ. The lifting up of Christ then, and now, would not suffice for those who lived before His death. What about those persons who lived before the death of Christ and died in their sins? They cannot be drawn. "If I be lifted up from the earth" teaches the *manner* of Christ's death; "will draw all men unto me" (from among Gentiles as well as Jews) explains the *fruit* of His death.

There is a *difference between "drawing and dragging."* The Greek words *suro* and *helkuo* differ. The Greek *surein* implies force or drag. When Saul made havoc of the church, he went into every house *dragging* both men and women and committing them to prison (Acts 8:3). The elect person is not to be likened to a fish that is hooked and dragged against its will, but he is drawn by the Divine attraction of God's love. "Draw me, we will run after thee: the king hath brought me into his chambers: we will be glad and rejoice in thee, we will remember thy love more than wine: the upright love thee" (S. of S. 1:4). The word for *draw* in John 6:44 is *helkuse.* The word here can mean no more than the elective force of love, attracting men to the Impeccable Saviour. "The Lord hath appeared of old unto me, saying, Yea, I have loved thee with an everlasting love: therefore *with lovingkindness have I drawn thee*" (Jer. 31:3).

The depraved sinner cannot, in his own strength, come to Christ. Professing Christendom's concept of the sinner is that he must "give his heart to Christ" if the blood of the Cross is to avail for his sins. This is accomplished by the sinner coming to Christ and "taking his stand for Christ." Thus, according to professing Christendom's concept of salvation, the finished work of Christ is left contingent on the fickle will of man as to whether it shall be a success or a failure. Their philosophy is that the sinner takes the first step and God does the rest; the sinner believes; then, God comes in and saves him. *This concept of salvation is a denial of the Spirit's work altogether.* If the sinner can get by without the Spirit's help at the beginning, he should have no difficulty getting along without Him the rest of the way. The Scriptures state: " . . . God hath from the beginning chosen you to salvation *through sanctification of the Spirit* and belief of the truth" (II Thess. 2:13). "Seeing ye have purified your souls in *obeying the truth through the Spirit* unto unfeigned love of the brethren . . . " (I Pet. 1:22).

The application of salvation is by the power of the Holy Spirit. The *fountain of regeneration* is the everlasting love of the Father (Jer. 31:3) ; the *procuring cause* is the atonement of Jesus Christ (Rom. 5:8-11) ; the *communication* of the Father's love through the substitutionary death of Christ is by the Holy Spirit (John 3:8). In Christ's discourse with Nicodemus, He used the *wind* as an illustration of the *efficient cause of salvation.* There are three important things to be considered in this illustration. (1) As the wind blows *freely,* not at the command of any creature, so the Spirit applies salvation to whom He will. The will of the Spirit is the same will of the Father and the Son. God and man stand in such relation to each other that they cannot both possess *free wills* in the same action. Only God has free will in the absolute sense. Man's will is free to go in only one direction like an automobile going down hill without brakes. Man's will, therefore, can be changed only by coming into contact with a Superior will; this is done by the drawing power of God. (2) As there is something in the wind which can be *heard,* proving its reality, so there is something in salvation which proves its reality. That which is *heard* in regeneration is the *effectual call.* "It is written in the prophets, And they shall be all taught of God. *Every man therefore that hath heard,* and hath learned of the Father, cometh unto me" (John 6:45). Thus the Holy Spirit makes the passive sinner active for the effectual call. The sinner is not absolutely passive at the time of his regeneration, but he is passive only with respect to spiritual things (Rom. 8:7; I Cor. 2:14). There must first be the presence of God in movement upon the sinner before there can be any movement of the sinner toward Christ. (3) As there is something *incomprehensible* about the wind, so there is something incomprehensible about salvation. Even in the natural kingdom the mystery of life and its origin are beyond our knowledge. After the origin of life, however, the development can be explained in a measure; but the inception that precedes all else is unknown.

The invitation, "Come unto me, all ye that labour and are heavy laden, and I will give you rest" (Matt. 11:28), must be studied in the light of the preceding verse. "All things are delivered unto me of my Father; and no man knoweth the Son, but the Father; neither knoweth any man the Father, save the Son, and *he to whomsoever the Son will reveal him"* (Matt. 11:27). This proves that men can only come to know God through the Lord Jesus Christ. The promise does not state that Christ will reveal the Father to everyone without exception, but only to those who *labour* and are *heavy laden.* Those who labour are persons who feel the burden of sin, and the heavy laden are those who feel the weight of that load. Since there is pleasure in sin (Heb. 11:25), there can never be a sense of *guilt* and *weight* of sin until there has been Divine conviction.

The depraved sinner is unable, without the help of God, to heed Christ's invitation. "No man can come to me, except the Father which hath sent me draw him ... " (John 6:44). This proves that no man can come to Christ by faith unless God draws him. How is the sinner drawn? *He is drawn by being taught of God.* His being taught of God is not merely an ascent of the mind but a serious apprehension of Divine truth in the heart. Everyone, therefore, who comes to Christ has been given a *hearing ear.* "The hearing ear, and the seeing eye, the Lord hath made even both of them" (Prov. 20:12). There are three great truths set forth in the following order: the *beginning,* the Father draws the elect sinner; the *progress,* the elect sinner hears and learns; and the *end,* the elect sinner comes to Christ. To whom does the phrase "all taught of God" refer? "All that the Father giveth me shall come to me" (John 6:37). How do we reconcile Matthew 11:28 with John 6:44? They need no reconciliation; there is blessed harmony between them.

Conditional and unconditional promises of God must be distinguished. The *conditional promise* calls for repentance. " ... And the times of this ignorance God winked at; but now commandeth all men everywhere to repent" (Acts 17:30). This command to repent does not suppose that men have power to turn from their sins to God. Why does God command men to do something they cannot do? Suppose a person absconded some money from his employer; would his employer not have the right to demand payment even though the thief did not have it to pay? Has not God, Who has been offended by sinful man, the right to command repentance even though the sinner is unable, because of his depravity, to turn in repentance to God? Man, by his depraved nature, has not the power to obey God; but God, by His sovereignty, has authority to command.

Man's hope is in the *unconditional promise* which gives repentance. " ... Then hath God also to the Gentiles *granted repentance unto life*" (Acts 11:18). This is not an external repentance, but repentance unto life. When God commands *all men* to repent, it is to show every man his need of repentance; and that he may, like Ephraim, apply to God for it. Ephraim, bemoaning himself, said, " ... turn thou me, and I shall be turned; for thou art the Lord my God. Surely after that I was turned, I repented ... " (Jer. 31:18,19). This repentance is not, like Pharaoh's, out of *desperation* (Ex. 9:29). The moving principle in Pharaoh's heart was not the power of God, but fear for his life. He was convinced of danger, but he was not convinced of God's righteousness. Saving repentance is not, like Ahab's, a *reformation* (I Kings 21:27). There is no record that Ahab reproved Jezebel for the murder of Naboth nor for failure to restore the vineyard to his family. He did not leave his idols; therefore, his reformation arose from dread of punishment and not from the fear of God.

The *conditional promise* calls for faith. Paul said to the Philippian jailor, "...Believe on the Lord Jesus Christ, and thou shalt be saved..." (Acts 16:31). God's *unconditional promise* gives the faith by which the sinner embraces Christ. Saving faith, which is a living faith, is wrought in man by the operation of the Holy Spirit. Paul calls the Holy Spirit the Spirit of faith (II Cor. 4:13), and in Galatians he mentions faith as the fruit of the Spirit (Gal. 5:22). Thus, saving faith is not the working of a faculty inherent in the natural man but something imparted to the natural man by the power of God (John 6:29; Eph. 2:8; Phil. 1:29).

The grace of God is irresistible, not because it drags men to Christ against their will but because it changes man's heart so that he comes most freely, for he is made willing by grace. *The sinner, apart from Divine help, is unable to be willing and unwilling to be able.*

The religious world is full of people *who put themselves between God and their salvation.* They believe that salvation is accomplished through the combined efforts of God and man. They believe that God takes the initiative in that He has provided salvation for everyone, but man's response is the determining factor because he is free to accept or reject God's offer of grace. At the crucial point, therefore, man's will plays a decisive role; thus man, not God, determines who will be the recipient of the gift of salvation.

The salvation of God is accomplished by the power of the Triune God. The Father chose a people, the Son died for them, and the Holy Spirit makes Christ's death effective by bringing the elect to repentance and faith, thereby, causing them to be willing to obey the gospel. *Thus God, not man, determines who will be the recipients of the gift of salvation.*

CHRIST'S DISCRIMINATING MESSAGE

The discriminating message of our Lord is Grace. It is called "the election of grace" (Rom. 11:5). "All that the Father giveth me shall come to me; and him that cometh to me I will in no wise cast out" (John 6:37). "But I tell you of a truth, *many widows* were in Israel in the days of Elias, . . . But unto none of them was Elias sent, *save* unto Sarepta, a city of Sidon, *unto a woman* that was a widow. And *many lepers* were in Israel in the time of Eliseus the prophet; and *none of them was cleansed, saving Naaman* the Syrian" (Luke 4:25-27). Grace reigns ". . . through righteousness unto eternal life by Jesus Christ our Lord" (Rom. 5:21). *Responsibility* came into this world in Adam, a peccable person whom Satan could touch. Adam was touched by Satan, and he fell with all his posterity in him. *Grace* came into this world in the Second Adam. The impeccable Christ stands invulnerable and invincible before every attack of Satan. The Son of God was manifested for the purpose of the reign of grace, and for this to be accomplished He destroyed the works of the Devil (I John 3:8).

Grace has always seemed like an insult to the natural man. It cannot seem otherwise since its principle design is to *mortify the pride of man and display the glory of Christ.* The grace of God which brings salvation does not look for righteousness from the sinner, but gives it to him. Grace is more than an *objective fact* presented to man; it is a *subjective experience* wrought by the Holy Spirit within the recipient. This subjective experience is not produced by our will, but by the "faith of the operation of God" (Col. 2:12). "For unto you it is *given* in the behalf of Christ, not only *to believe* on him, but also to suffer for his sake" (Phil. 1:29). The Psalmist, recognizing the sovereignty of God in salvation, said, "Blessed is the man whom thou *choosest, and causest to approach unto thee,* that he may dwell in thy courts . . ." (Ps. 65:4).

A general proclamation of grace does not disturb people; natural men despise grace illustrated. The real character of grace is not known until it is illustrated. As soon as the Saviour displayed grace by the illustrations of the "woman of Sidon" and of "Naaman the Syrian" (Luke 4:25-27), the people were "filled with wrath"

(Luke 4:28). The wrath of Christ's enemies was so excited that they rose up ". . . and thrust him out of the city, and led him unto the brow of the hill whereon their city was built, that they might cast him down headlong" (Luke 4:29). This anger has not subsided. Men cannot now cast Christ out of their cities, but they do exclude Him from their religion. All the cry of our day against discrimination is, in reality, a manifestation of opposition against the discriminating God of the Bible. The reason for such manifestation of wrath is that grace will not acknowledge the righteousness of man but blesses him in spite of his unrighteousness. Calvary is the religious world's answer to grace, but it is God's answer to heaven's justice and love. Grace reigns through the righteousness of God which has fulfilled the law, satisfied justice, and displayed holiness.

Grace is God's *eternal choice* of some in Christ to be saved. "According as he *hath chosen* us in him before the foundation of the world . . ." (Eph. 1:4). The electing God does not eliminate the Person and work of Jesus Christ. "But we are bound to give thanks alway to God for you, brethren beloved of the Lord, because God *hath from the beginning chosen you to salvation* through sanctification of the Spirit and belief of the truth: Whereunto he called you by our gospel, to the obtaining of the glory of our Lord Jesus Christ" (II Thess. 2:13,14). Election is set within the context of a doxology (Rom. 9-11). There was neither the error of activism nor passivism with Paul in regard to God's absolute sovereignty; he saw the way of salvation in the light of sovereign election. Paul was led to understand that his salvation was not of works but of God's grace, and in the election by God he found a peace that passed all understanding.

There are two dangers in the study of Divine election: *activism* and *passivism*. Truth has always been surrounded by extremes of error, and the truth of election is no different. Activism is a restless zeal that has been excited to opposition because Divine election finds in the best nothing to attract and in the worst nothing to deter. Passivism, the other extreme, is the concept of election that eliminates the means to the Divinely appointed end.

Those who believe in an "elected plan" of salvation have the same concept of God in soteriology (science of salvation) that deists have of God in theology (science of God). The deist does not deny a transcendent God; he believes that God is the Maker and Sustainer of a world which, by its order and design, points to its eternal and all-wise Creator. On the other hand, the deist accepts the fact of nature; he believes that nature possesses a fixed constitution and operates according to unalterable laws. It would appear that within this scheme the worshiper and the investigator can both find a togetherness, but they cannot because such dualism excludes any idea of miracle. Thus, God is excluded from nature except at the point of origin. There is no place for providence to penetrate nature because all that happens in it is of its own fixed properties.

The same deistic philosophy is found in the realm of soteriology —the science of salvation. For example, it is said, "God elected a plan of salvation which He accomplished in Christ. Man may either reject or accept this plan." Do we not constantly hear it said that God has done all that He can, and now it is up to the sinner? This is deistic soteriology. This excludes God from salvation except in its plan and origin. The elected plan idea eliminates God from its application, denying the miracle of the new birth wrought by the power of the Spirit. "And when the Gentiles heard this, they were glad, and glorified the word of the Lord: and *as many as were ordained to eternal life believed*" (Acts 13:48). This is an ordination, not to an office nor to the means of grace but to grace and glory itself. According to Ephesians 1:3-14, each Person of the Godhead has a part in the salvation of the sinner. The Father's part was to *choose and plan;* the Son's part was to *prove and provide;* the Spirit's part is to *apply and seal.*

The advocates of an "elected plan" omit God altogether from the application of salvation. They make the will of God dependent on the will of man. This makes the will of man the sovereign will because they say that God has done all that He can. Their inconsistency is evident in such a statement as, "Man by his free will may accept or reject God's sovereign will." Man's free will, in this statement, is given power over God's sovereign will; therefore, God's sovereignty must, by necessity, be limited sovereignty. If God's sovereignty is limited, then He is not the sovereign God of the Bible. In order for the propagators of an "elected plan" of salvation to be consistent, they must encourage people to pray not to God but to the sinner.

What is the connection between the will of God and the will of man? What is the relation between them? What is the order in which they stand to each other? The will of God is the will which is altogether absolute and independent; therefore, His will is the first, not the second, in movement. Even the renewed will follows; it does not lead (Phil. 2:12,13). An unholy will cannot follow because it is not bent in the direction of God but Satan. "Ye will not come to me, that ye might have life" (John 5:40). The depraved will of man is bent toward Satan and must be changed by God. God's prerogative is to bestow "mercy on whom He will" (Rom. 9:15). "So then it is not of him that willeth, nor of him that runneth, but of God that sheweth mercy" (Rom. 9:16).

Many become passive when they see that nothing can be done to change God's will. This concept of Divine election leads to an attitude that is antimissionary and a denial of ordained means to an ordained end. Election, however, does not eliminate either the gospel or the work of the Holy Spirit in regeneration. The measure of our duty is God's command, not our ability. Though we cannot save ourselves, we can come to the pool; though we cannot understand spiritual things, we can read the Word of God; though we cannot cleanse ourselves, we can cry, "Lord, if thou wilt, thou canst make me clean."

The Bible teaches that men are brought to believe on Jesus Christ; but God, not man, sends the messengers and determines the recipients. When the gospel of Christ is proclaimed to an audience, that audience from one point of view is undifferentiated. In this respect, all the members are alike in their depravity; therefore, there is no spiritual receptivity. From another viewpoint, those who hear the Word are differentiated because God gives the "hearing ear" (Prov. 20:12). While the preaching of the gospel of Christ is general, the content of the preaching is particular.

There are two kinds of promises taught in the Scriptures: *conditional* and *unconditional*. In a conditional promise, the recipient fulfills the conditions of the promise before receiving the blessing. This is a promise with an *if* attached; it is not absolute. There is no *condition* nor *if* attached to an unconditional promise; it is absolute. The conditional promise is not always fulfilled because of the unfaithfulness of man; the unconditional promise must be fulfilled because of the faithfulness of God.

The promise in John 6:37 is unconditional. "All that the Father giveth me shall come to me; and him that cometh to me I will in no wise cast out." God's promise to Abraham, "Sarah thy wife *shall* bear thee a son" (Gen. 17:19; 18:10), was an unconditional promise. How could Sarah have a son since she was passed age? The reason was God gave an unconditional promise. Isaac's coming into the world could not be attributed to anything either in Abraham or Sarah; his coming, therefore, was attributed to the sovereign God Who promised and Whose promise had enough virtue in it to accomplish the thing promised.

The unconditional promise God made to Abraham concerning a son was not disproved by Abraham's faith. Abraham had faith, but his faith was of such nature that it did not consider either the deadness of his body or of Sarah's womb (Rom. 4:19,20). Natural faith would have considered the deadness of both; but faith, which is the gift of God, is the substance of things hoped for, the evidence of things not seen (Heb. 11:1). Had Abraham looked on any *natural means,* he would have *staggered;* but he looked only to the power of Him Who promised. This is the only faith that can glorify God; it is faith in God ". . . who quickeneth the dead and calleth those things which be not as though they were" (Rom. 4:17). No difficulty can stand in the way of such faith. Natural faith looks to the will of the sinner; supernatural faith looks to the will of God. Natural faith looks to the ability of the sinner to come to Christ; supernatural faith looks to the ability of God Who draws the sinner to Christ. Natural faith makes the will of God dependent on the will of the sinner; supernatural faith makes the will of the sinner dependent on the will of God. Such faith, which is the gift of God, accepts the fact that God is the Author and Finisher of our salvation in Christ.

Abraham believed "God who quickeneth the dead" (Rom. 4:17). He comprehended the fact that life was of God, and that God could do as He pleased in matters of life and death. The word *quicken* means to make alive, to endue with life, to produce life, or to make alive with Christ (Eph. 2:1; Col. 2:13). Abraham had to learn, before he experienced life coming from his dead loins (the seat of generative power, Heb. 7:5,10), the meaning of death. He believed that God was able to bring life out of his dead loins. God would, therefore, bring Isaac into existence in the same fashion as when He said in the midst of darkness, "Let there be light: and there was light." So now in the midst of Abraham's dead loins and Sarah's dead womb, God said, "Let there be Isaac: and there was Isaac." Thus, He called Isaac, who was not, as though he were.

When God makes an unconditional promise, the fulfillment of the promise does not exist at the time it is made. The guarantee of its fulfillment exists at the time the promise is made; otherwise, God would be a liar. "God is not a man, that he should lie; neither the son of man that he should repent; hath he said, and shall he not do it? or hath he spoken, and shall he not make it good?" (Num. 23:19). Isaac was a child of an unconditional promise; therefore, he was born, fulfilling the promise to Abraham.

All who come to Christ for salvation are the children of promise. "Now, we, brethen, as Isaac was, are the children of promise" (Gal. 4:28). They are not like Ishmael who was the son of Hagar, the slave woman; they are like Isaac who was born of Sarah, the free woman. Since Isaac was the son of Sarah, he was not the son of flesh but of promise. All who come to Christ know that their salvation is not in the usual course of nature, but it is miraculously accomplished by the promise and power of God. The Lord Jesus said, "All that the Father giveth me shall come to me; and him that cometh to me I will in no wise cast out" (John 6:37). Are not all who come to Christ the children of promise? Is not the word *shall* the same guarantee of salvation to those *given* to Christ as the word *shall* was the guarantee of Isaac being born of Abraham? No one but a spiritually blind person would deny that the word *shall* refers to an absolute promise.

It cannot be denied that the Father *gave some* to Christ to save. "As thou hast given him power over all flesh, that he should give eternal life to as many as thou hast given him" (John 17:2). The *as many* that the Father gave to Christ will be the same *as many* that shall believe on Christ (Acts 13:48; Rom. 8:28-30). How are they given to Christ? They are given by the electing God, and the gift was before the foundation of the world (Eph. 1:4; II Tim. 1:9). The as many *elected* or *given* can never be twisted to mean "a plan"; as many and "a plan" cannot, by any stretch of the imagination, mean the same thing. The objects of election are persons, not "a plan." No person can, unless given to Christ, believe; for Christ said, "But ye believe not, because *ye are not my sheep,* as I said unto you. *My sheep hear my voice,* and I know them, and *they* follow me: And I give unto *them* eternal life; and *they* shall never perish . . ." (John 10:26-28). How can the plural words, *sheep, they,* and *them,* be made to mean "plan" which is singular?

All that the Father elected in Christ *shall come* to Christ. But how shall they come if they are dead? The word *shall* is confined to "all that are given to Christ." Therefore, the *shall come* makes their coming not only the gift of the Father but the purpose of the Son. Christ is obligated to communicate the Spirit of grace to the elect, thus, causing them to come. They shall come not if they will (John 5:40), but by the will and power of God they are made willing (Ps. 110:3). If the sinner's salvation is dependent on his repentance and faith apart from the power of God, then there can be no certainty of its accomplishment. As God quickened the dead loins of Abraham and the dead womb of Sarah for the production of life, so He quickens dead sinners. "And you hath he quickened (made alive), who were dead in trespasses and sins" (Eph. 2:1). The salvation of the elect is so related to the Divine purpose that it cannot fail. *Shall come* can raise the dead, heal the leper, cure the impotent, or give sight to the blind. Thus, the dead *shall* rise, the leper *shall* be cleansed, the lame *shall* walk, the blind *shall* see, and the elect sinner *shall* come to Christ.

The elect come to Christ because they were elected "in Christ." "According as he hath chosen us in him" (Eph. 1:4). The election of Jesus Christ was the first and chief election. "Behold my servant, whom I uphold; mine elect, in whom my soul delighteth . . ." (Is. 42:1). "To whom coming, as unto a living stone, disallowed indeed of men, but chosen of God, and precious" (I Pet. 2:4). He was chosen first and set up as the Head, and then His people were chosen in Him. He was chosen to be the Saviour of the elect, and the elect were appointed to salvation in Him. "For God hath not appointed us to wrath, but to obtain salvation by our Lord Jesus Christ" (I Thess. 5:9). The Lord Jesus was ordained to be the Saviour (I Pet. 1:20). He was to be the Saviour of a chosen number, and that number shall come to Christ by faith. Faith does not produce election, but election produces faith (Acts 13:48). We come to Christ for salvation because God said that we *shall come;* we shall come because it is *given* us to come. God said, ". . . I have spoken it, I will also bring it to pass; I have purposed it, I will also do it" (Is. 46:11).

CHRIST'S MIRACLES

Miracles were signs of attestation. "Ye men of Israel, hear these words; Jesus of Nazareth, a man approved of God among you by miracles and wonders and signs ..." (Acts 2:22). "Believe me that I am in the Father, and the Father in me: or else believe me for the very works' sake" (John 14:11). God never wrought miracles to gratify curiosity, but *to prove that His power was Divine.* A greater manifestation of power may be expected at the creation of the world or at the commencement of an age than during the continuance of either. A miracle is God's omnipotence becoming a scaffold on which to plant God's truth. When the building of Truth is complete, the scaffold is removed. This is what Paul meant when he said, "Charity never faileth: but whether there be prophecies, they shall fail; whether there be tongues, they shall cease; whether there be knowledge, it shall vanish away" (I Cor. 13:8). Paul explained miraculous gifts to the Corinthians by showing the difference between that which endures forever and the things which serve their purpose in a given period of time.

The extraordinary gifts of prophecy, tongues, and knowledge passed away when that which was perfect came (I Cor. 13:10). When the apostle John wrote the book of Revelation, the apostolic age ended; consequently, the Bible was finished, and the Word of God had been fully confirmed by the miracles of God through the apostles. "Truly the signs of an apostle were wrought among you in all patience, in signs, and wonders, and mighty deeds" (II Cor. 12:12). "How shall we escape, if we neglect so great salvation, which at the first began to be spoken by the Lord, and was *confirmed* unto us by them that heard him; God also bearing them witness, both with signs and wonders, and with divers miracles, and gifts of the Holy Ghost, according to his own will?" (Heb. 2:3,4). We have now come to the age when apostolic miracles are no more needed than the sacrifices of the Old Testament. As the purpose of sacrifices has been fulfilled by the One Perfect Sacrifice of Christ, so the purpose of apostolic miracles has been fulfilled by the completion of the Bible—"the perfect law of liberty" (James 1:25).

Christ's miracles have a redemptive character. When Jesus Christ healed the sick and raised the dead, He manifested His sovereign power over the spiritual poverty of depraved humanity. When He fed the thousands with a few loaves and fishes, He demonstrated His ability to reverse the curse of barrenness caused by the fall. When He walked upon the yielding waves and beckoned to the obedient winds, He showed that He was creation's Lord; therefore, He would, in time to come, make all things new. His works and miracles bear the stamp of Redeemer—the evidence of redemptive power. His miracles in the physical realm were examples of what He had come to do in the spiritual.

The recorded miracles of our Lord, during His earthly ministry, have a progressive character. His changing water into wine showed Himself the God of nature; healing the sick revealed power over disease; the miraculous catch of fish manifested control over the animate creation; casting out the devil proved ability over demons; raising the dead displayed control over death and decay. The progressive character of His miracles gives a wonderful illustration of His power and grace in the salvation of sinners.

Our Lord came to preach deliverance to the captives. He came to set the prisoner free but left John the Baptist to die in Herod's prison. Herod's birthday was John's death-day (Mark 6:14-29). No Christian doubts Christ's ability to put down all tyrants and deliver His people; nevertheless, they are all ordained of God for the fulfillment of His purpose. "Surely the wrath of man shall praise thee: the remainder of wrath shalt thou restrain" (Ps. 76:10). The Lord wants His people to know that the world's pleasure often proves to be their trouble, but God is glorified in their trouble. We need not assume that just because we are endeavoring to walk in the ways of God we shall be exempt from the troubles which afflict the saints of God in various ways. Paul said, "We are troubled on every side . . ." (II Cor. 4:8). David prayed, "Have mercy upon me, O Lord, consider my trouble which I suffer of them that hate me . . ." (Ps. 9:13). Steadfast faith in time of trouble evidences a token of God's righteousness. Such heroic endurance is so unusual as to indicate its Divine source. Therefore, they are sure to be delivered; their enemies are sure to be punished because justice is justice and God is God (II Thess. 1:7-10). The deliverance of the elect from sin does not guarantee their deliverance from, but through, trouble.

There was a *great multitude* of impotent folk at the pool of

Bethesda (John 5), but *Christ healed only one man*. Among this great multitude there was a *certain man* to whom the Saviour said, "Wilt *thou* be made whole?" The record states that "the impotent *man* took up his bed and walked." Christ took the first step in the impotent man's healing. Bethesda was crowded with people, but the Son of God was not recognized by the multitude. *The Light shined in darkness, but the darkness comprehended not the Light.* There is no difference today. Man does not discover his need of Christ by natural discernment, nor does he come to Christ by natural strength and will. Bethesda is a vivid description of the cumbersome machinery of human religion while the grace of God is rejected. As the Son of God manifests His sovereignty by healing only *one man* out of the multitude, so He reveals His sovereignty in salvation by saving only the *elect* out of the multitudes.

The first advent of Christ was not for the purpose of banishing tyranny and death. He did not proclaim universal healing, liberty to all captives, nor resurrection of all the dead. We affirm that *the Impeccable Saviour was able to do all these things;* but deny that He actually healed all the sick, set at liberty all the captives, and *raised all the dead.*

Many religious people have more zeal than knowledge; their main emphasis is the miraculous works of Christ rather than His Impeccable Person. Crowds of people speak of physical healing to the neglect of the spiritual; they gather around *modern Bethesdas*. John gives the true order of healing. "Beloved, I wish above all things that thou mayest prosper and be in health, even as thy soul prospereth" (III John 2). A message on the Impeccable Saviour holds very little, if any, interest to these religionists. Physical healing occupies their chief interest. Their philosophy is similar to that of people who desire to be saved from the punishment of hell, but desire no part of the Lordship of Christ. They want the blessing but not the Blesser.

Failure to ascertain the true sense of Scripture is a danger among religionists. They think a mere quotation of Scripture is sufficient to prove their point and silence all opponents. These people give no consideration to the relevance of Scripture which they quote; the context is completely ignored. Others suppose it would be a perversion or denial of Scripture to place a different meaning upon what appears to be its obvious sense. For example, they think that such statements as "this is my body" (John 6:50-58; Matt. 26:26-28) or "out of his belly shall flow rivers of living water" (John 7:38) must be understood *literally. Scripture requires interpretation;* and only when the Word is handled aright, can the truth be known. As the prophets did not speak apart from being *borne along by the Spirit* (II Pet. 1:20, 21), so Christians can never know the true meaning of Scripture apart from the *illumination of the Holy Spirit* (I Cor. 2:9-14).

The Saviour proved His resurrection power by raising Lazarus from the dead (John 11:43). If Jesus Christ had not called Lazarus by name, all the dead would have come forth. During this age of grace, the voice of the Saviour is heard by those whom He calls by name. ". . . the sheep hear his voice: and he calleth his own sheep by name, and leadeth them out. And when he putteth forth his own sheep, he goeth before them, and the sheep follow him, for they know his voice" (John 10:3,4). The sovereignty of God is displayed in the calling, by name, of the dead in sin. But He does not call all the dead in sin to life. "Verily, verily, I say unto you, the hour is coming, *and now is,* when *the dead shall hear* the voice of the Son of God: and *they that hear shall live*" (John 5:25). The day will come when the dead bodies in their graves shall be resurrected. ". . . the hour is coming, in the which all that are in the graves shall hear his voice. And shall come forth, they that have done good, unto the resurrection of life; and they that have done evil, unto the resurrection of damnation" (John 5:28,29). *Christ does not call all without exception to salvation,* but He does call all without exception to judgment—the saved to the "judgment seat of Christ" (II Cor. 5:10) and the unsaved to the "great white throne" (Rev. 20:11).

Miraculous power was exercised to accredit the testimony of the apostles (II Cor. 12:12). We cannot, however, isolate one incident of miraculous power from the other experiences of Paul. The miraculous power which opened the Philippian jail (Acts 16:25-36) for Paul was not displayed in other prison experiences. Why did he not appeal for miraculous intervention as he stood before Caesar? The foremost champion of miracles now stood alone. "At my first answer no man stood with me, but all men forsook me: I pray God that it may not be laid to their charge" (II Tim. 4:16).

What is the answer to the absence of miraculous signs in this age of grace? *Christianity is not received on the authority of miracles.* Did not the people who witnessed Christ's miracles crucify Him as an imposter? God's silence now is because the climax of Divine revelation has been reached. No disciple of Christ ever attributed his faith to the ground of miracles. Everything must be tested by the "perfect law of liberty" (James 1:25). Consider carefully what our Lord said at the passover feast in Jerusalem! "Now when he was in Jerusalem at the passover, in the feast day, many believed in his name, *when they saw the miracles* which he did. But *Jesus did not commit himself unto them,* because he knew all men" (John 2:23,24). Thus, we see that men's affections may be stirred and intellects informed, but Christ will not commit Himself unto stony ground hearers (Matt. 13:5,6).

The God of the Bible is a miracle working God, but one of the great mysteries of our age is not the occurrence but absence of miracles. We must consider *what God is doing;* not merely what He has done or will do. One cannot deny that Christ is now on the Father's throne, and all power in heaven and earth is His. Therefore, Christ could, if it were in His plan, do for men today all that He did for them in the days of His flesh. Nevertheless, the fact remains it is not a matter of the Lord's ability but of His plan for men of this age. Christ did not come primarily to be a miracle worker in the sense of healing the sick, stilling the storm, and raising the dead. His miracles were credentials for His claims of Deity. His character does not change (Heb. 13:8; Mal. 3:6), but His *method* does. God is no longer demanding animal sacrifices in worship, but He does demand the "sacrifice of praise" (Heb. 13:15).

The age of grace is not the time when more miraculous power needs to be performed, but more grace evidenced through Christians. Christianity exhorts men not to covet great demonstrations of miraculous gifts (I Cor. 12) by which to dazzle people; but to covet earnestly the *best gifts* of faith, hope, and charity (I Cor. 12:31; 13:13). Some people are like the nobleman who besought Christ to heal his son (John 4:46-54). Christ said unto him. ". . . Except ye see signs and wonders, ye will not believe" (John 4:48). The man was demanding signs of Christ before he would trust his boy's case into the Lord's hands. God will not be dictated to by man, for He is the sovereign Lord. Faith, which is the gift of God, does not need signs and wonders. Lame faith looks for crutches of miraculous signs. "A wicked and adulterous generation seeketh after a sign; and there shall no sign be given unto it, but the sign of the prophet Jonas ... " (Matt. 16:4). Here is the standard by which faith is measured. This determines whether it is true or lame.

Paul's sufferings revealed a greater degree of faith than the mighty deeds of his earlier ministry. It was not until he entered on the *path of faith,* as we know it now, that his life became ". . . a pattern to them which should hereafter believe on him (Christ) to life everlasting" (I Tim. 1:16). To believe in Christ is to own His Lordship now; in the power of this truth Christians live and die. Thus, the miracle of regeneration gives the faith of perseverence.

There is a threefold reason why Christ did not, in His first advent, banish sickness, tyranny, and death. They are (1) The redemption of the body is not yet; we still wait for it. ". . . even we ourselves groan within ourselves, waiting for the adoption, to wit, the redemption of our body" (Rom. 8:23). Christ's redemptive work is absolutely perfect and finished—Godward—so that *"He* is the propitiation for our sins," but its application to our bodies remains to be accomplished. (2) The day of righteous government is not yet. We look forward to the time when "the government shall be upon his shoulder . . ." (Is. 9:6). Christ is the *"King of righteousness"* before He is the *"King of peace"* (Heb. 7:2). Tyrants still hold their cruel sway, but they are overruled to serve God's eternal purpose. Tyrants, however, will be ruled with a rod of iron during the righteous reign of peace and prosperity which is to come. (3) The day when all that are in their graves shall come forth is not yet. The resurrection of both the just and the unjust is future.

CHRIST'S DEATH

God sent His Son into the world to manifest what He *would do* as God, not what He *could do* as the Impeccable Man. It is impossible to separate Christ's Person from His work. Paul said to the Corinthians, "For I determined not to know anything among you, *save Jesus Christ, and him crucified*" (I Cor. 2:2). There is such an inseparable connection between His Person and work that any separation would result in heresy; there would be a wrong concept of both His Person and work. The gospel desires that we understand what Jesus Christ has done for sinners, but not at the expense of Who He is. If His Person were not understood, man would only be puzzled by His work and ask, ". . . Whence hath this man this wisdom, and these mighty works? Is not this the carpenter's son? is not his mother called Mary? and his brethren, James, and Joses, and Simon, and Judas? And his sisters, are they not all with us? Whence then hath this man all these things? And they were offended in him . . ." (Matt. 13:54-57).

A self-made concept of Christ is dangerous. This danger is illustrated by Israel desiring to take Christ, whom they thought to be a prophet, and make Him King (John 6:14,15). This desire of Israel issued from seeing Christ's miraculous work (John 6:1-14). Let us not be misled by those who seem to honor Christ! As Jesus Christ would not commit Himself unto some who believed in His name because He knew what was in them (John 2:23-25), so our blessed Lord will not commit Himself unto those who extoll a peccable Christ because He knows what is in their hearts. God commits Himself subjectively only to those who by revelation embrace the objective fact concerning the Person of Christ.

What was the nature of the incarnation? There are those who hold the idea of "incarnation even without a fall." This thought holds to the supposition that the incarnation would have taken place even if Adam had not fallen by reason of his sin. Such speculation is far removed from Biblical evidence. Modern thought is that God acted only because man, in rebellion, acted first. This makes God's action to follow, rather than sovereignly precede, human action. The Bible teaches that God's plan to gather all together in His Son did not originate at the time of the fall, but from eternity (Eph. 1:3-11). Christ's redemptive work was not something which happened by accident in the course of human history, but something which took place in eternity according to God's eternal purpose (Eph. 3:11). The incarnation is to be viewed in historical unity with the cross (Gal. 4:4; Rom. 8:3; Heb. 10:7-14).

The eternal purpose of God is not a lifeless command. Most of the difficulty derived from God's eternal purpose is caused by a misunderstanding of eternity. Eternity is *present* and *future* as well as *past*. Eternity must not be thought of merely as past and future, but also as present. The blood of the eternal covenant (Heb. 13:20) must not be contemplated as something related only to the present, but to the past and future. This covenant *accompanies* and *follows* as well as *precedes* its fulfillment. It cannot be regarded as a lifeless foreordination.

The eternal purpose of God is related to the eternal Son of God. The election of God is not to be sought in the hidden counsel of God, but in the Word of God (Deut. 29:29). The Lord Jesus is Author, Object, and Substance of Biblical revelation. The eternal election of God is to be sought in Christ because only in Him can one's predestination be known (Eph. 1:3-5).

The purpose of God is a unity. It is the establishment of the eternal covenant with a chosen people as fulfilled in the redemptive work of the Lamb slain from the foundation of the world (Rev. 13:8). God's eternal purpose carries with it other general purposes just as the unity of God includes a great number of perfections. As the perfections of God are all one in will and purpose, so the general purposes of God concerning the elect are all encompassed within the framework of the eternal purpose which He purposed in Christ Jesus (Eph. 3:11).

The word purpose (Eph. 3:11), like doctrine (II John 9), is singular. As God has but one all inclusive plan, so He has but one doctrine concerning that plan. The eternal purpose of God so far transcends the finite mind of man that he cannot comprehend it but after the manner of man. The conditions of man such as *before* and *after* the fall are not in the Divine mind as they are in ours. Man thinks successively, but God thinks simultaneously. If there were succession in God, He could not be the I AM; He could not call those things that be not as though they are (Rom. 4:17).

The concepts of supralapsarianism and infralapsarianism are nothing but human conceptions. The word *lapsarian* refers to the doctrine that man is a fallen creature. But there is much argument between the two major lapsarian views. The supra position says that God purposed to elect before He decreed to create man. Infra conviction states that God purposed to create before He decreed to elect. Does not the problem of order presuppose a transposition of the temporal into the eternity of God's counsel? Such a concept of succession in the Divine purpose is nothing short of humanizing God. We admit there is order in God's plan as there is order in the Godhead, but no one view can be primary because all are perfect. When the subject of eternity is properly apprehended, the subjects of election and creation will cease to be speculative guesses. There is one immutable purpose of God which encompasses every thing even to the number of hairs on a person's head (Matt. 10:30). This infinite understanding of God does not advance by degrees as man's, but by one act of the mind everything is simultaneously known.

The death of Christ cannot be dated from God's viewpoint because He is the Lamb slain from the foundation of the world (Rev. 13:8). Thus, the Lord Jesus was the Lamb slain: (1) *Determinately,* in the counsel of God (Acts 2:23) ; (2) *Promissorily,* in the Word of God (Gen. 3:15) ; (3) *Typically,* in the sacrifices appointed after the promise; (4) *Efficaciously,* in regard to its merit applied to believers before the actual death of Christ (Rom. 3:25; Heb. 9:15) ; (5) *Actually,* at the time of Christ's death (Heb. 9:15) ; (6) *Effectually,* in its application to repentant believers (Rom. 3:25) ; and (7) *Finally,* at the consummation of all things (Eph. 1:10; Rev. 21:5). These seven perfections of redemption are not contemplated by God as being successive, but they are observed by man as having come by degrees.

The value of Christ's death is based on His Person. Since God cannot die, we must understand that it was the humanity of Christ, the seed of Abraham, that was offered as a spotless sacrifice to God for the sins of believers (I Pet. 1:18-21). In order for Jesus Christ to qualify as Saviour, He must die for (1) *What man has done* (I John 3:5), (2) *What man has not done* (Rom. 3:23), and (3) *What man is by nature* (Eph. 2:3). Thus, the wrath due to man's *sins* and *sinful nature* was borne by the Impeccable

Saviour because He had neither a sinful nature nor acts of sin to disqualify Him. His perfect life qualified Him for the perfect sacrifice for *sins of nature*. His Impeccability qualified Him as the substitute for the *nature of sin*. It is nothing short of blasphemy to say that Jesus Christ could have sinned.

The death of Christ must minister satisfaction to God for sin. Finite man cannot make satisfaction, but Jesus Christ the God-Man made satisfaction. The Deity of Christ made it possible for Him to minister to God that which the Divine nature demanded. Christ's perfect human nature made it possible for Him to become the elect sinner's substitute. Thus, the Infinite Saviour stood in the place of all for whom He died and rendered satisfaction to the Infinite God. He filled up that void, made up that deficit, and restored that balance so ". . . God was in Christ, reconciling the world unto himself . . . " (II Cor. 5:19).

The satisfaction Christ made to God was a tremendous order. Let us observe this gigantic task from the commercial, legal, and moral views.

The commercial view of the debt of sin is often applied in Scripture. "Now to him that worketh is the reward not reckoned of grace, but of debt. But to him that worketh not, but believeth on him that justifieth the ungodly, his faith is counted for righteousness" (Rom. 4:4,5). The figure of debt is here employed. If we think about how much all the Christians who are alive owe, the sum is staggering. But carry this thought to include all the saints of the past, present, and future. Nurse that commercial figure in our minds for a moment and ask, "who can pay that debt?" Only an Infinite Person, out of His infinite resources, could pay such a debt.

The legal figure of sin's penalty is employed in the Bible. "For the wages of sin is death . . ." (Rom. 6:23). "Christ hath redeemed us from the curse of the law, being made a curse for us: for it is written, Cursed is every one that hangeth on a tree" (Gal. 3:13). Jesus Christ came to pay the law's penalty because His Deity gave Him an infinite capacity. No man could have endured the suffering for all the elect. For example, suppose a thousand men have been sentenced to receive one hundred lashes from a whip. No man could stand in the place of those one thousand sentenced men and receive their one hundred thousand lashes. Add to this number one thousand lashes for every person who shall enter heaven by virtue of Christ's death, and your mind will whirl. The Lord Jesus could not have suffered such agony in His own Person had not His Deity given Him an infinite capacity. We who are saved rejoice with Peter who said, "For Christ also hath once suffered for sins, the just for the unjust, that he might bring us to God . . . " (I Pet. 3:18).

Christ's moral nature, though absolutely perfect and infinitized by union with Deity, was wonderfully sensitive. Moral evil of sinners dulls the sensibilities until sin ceases to offend. This is witnessed on every hand today. Christians are made sensitive by grace; they are grateful for their sensitivity. Jesus Christ, however, was the most sensitive soul that ever walked this earth. This is easily understood since He breathed the atmosphere of Divine holiness and hated sin with an infinite hatred. The very advent of Christ into this earth corrupted by sin must have been torture to His infinitely sensitive nature. The perfection of Christ's moral sensibilities gave Him an infinite capacity for suffering.

The crowning text that proves the substitutionary value of Christ's death is Hebrews 9:14. "How much more shall the blood of Christ, who through the eternal Spirit offered himself without spot to God, purge your conscience from dead works to serve the living God." Substitution demanded a finished work which required death and brought life. This work was accomplished by the Trinity. The incarnate Son poured out His life through the Spirit of holiness for the satisfaction of God's justice. It was not the life which Jesus Christ lived that saves man, but *the life poured out in the shedding of blood*. The live lamb in the home of an Israelite could not save the older son from the judgment of the avenging angel, but the *slain lamb delivered him*. Sin can be seen in only two places, either on the sinner or Christ the substitute. The Impeccable Christ was offered without spot to God to purge the conscience of every person whose sins He bore (I Pet. 2:24). The dead works from which believers are purged are the operations of sin which came from spiritually dead souls (Eph. 2:1). It has been said that a will written with a dead man's hand will not stand up before the law. Thus, the living God can be served only by a person who has been made alive in Christ Jesus by the Spirit of regeneration.

The blood of the Cross justifies God as well as the repentant sinner. There is a mutual justification in the Cross of Christ. The righteousness of God is vindicated in admitting to His holy presence all sinners who experience the new birth. The blood of Christ, which was offered once in the end of the age, has both a retroactive and prospective value (Rom. 3:25; Heb. 9:15; Matt. 20:28). Some claim that it is not moral to forgive sinners without punishing their sin. God makes the same claim, and the claim is justified in the substitutionary work of Christ.

What is the *extent* of Christ's death? The nature of a ransom is such that when paid and accepted it automatically frees the person for whom it was intended. Justice demands that those for whom the ransom is paid shall be freed from any further obligation; it cannot demand the penalty twice.

Some teach that Christ died conditionally for all but absolutely for none. This is a God-dishonoring view of redemption; it makes Christ the purchaser of a redemption that is left to the power of man to render it effectual. By the obedience of Christ the gift of grace abounds to many; and by this One, Jesus Christ, righteousness reigns (Rom. 5:15-19). Man, therefore, has no part in this righteousness which reigns in life by One, Jesus Christ; it is not by two, Christ and man. *Christ's suretyship and sufferings are of the same extent; His sacrifice and intercession are related to the same persons.*

The Father's election, the Son's redemption, and the Spirit's regeneration are all of equal extent. Universal redemption would mean universal salvation. The fact is the Son redeems no more than the Father elects, and the Spirit regenerates no more than the Son redeems. ". . . the Son of man came not to be ministered unto, but to minister, and *to give his life a ransom for many*" (Matt. 20:28).

Many religionists are horrified by the term *limited redemption*. However, everyone limits redemption. It is limited either in its extent or in its quality. Those who say Christ died for every one without exception limit its quality (character) since the Bible states that many have and will die in their sins. The *extent* is limited by those who have a Biblical view of redemption. They dare not limit its character, but do admit that many die without experiencing salvation. Since every one limits redemption, the instructed Christian limits its extent and would never limit its character.

CHRIST'S HEADSHIP

Headship is the great principle of the moral universe. "But I would have you know, that the head of every man is Christ; and the head of the woman is the man; and the head of Christ is God" (I Cor. 11:3). The principle of order and subordination extends throughout the whole universe. Paul distinguishes between inferiority and subordination. For example, the Head of Christ is God; this is not in respect of essence but office. Christ is fulfilling the office of Mediator between God and man (I Tim. 2:5). The man is head of the woman, but not in respect of a different and more excellent nature; this is in regard to function because woman was made for man. The desire of Christ was ever toward His Head, God the Father. He said, ". . . for I do always those things that please him (the Father)" (John 8:29). The woman must, in order to carry out the Divine principle, find her desire in her husband. "Unto the woman he (God) said, I will greatly multiply thy sorrow and thy conception; in sorrow thou shalt bring forth children; and thy desire shall be to thy husband, and he shall rule over thee" (Gen. 3:16).

Paul proclaims the order which God established. This order is ever to be observed regardless of customs this godless age might exhibit. Our day is one in which both principle and order are being set aside by this evil and adulterous generation. The Christian, however, must never let down or compromise the principle or order of the Bible.

Headship has an important place in the ways of God. God has brought in One Who is entitled to be reverenced. He is the One whose every movement, *both inward and outward,* was in the spirit of obedience. He was the Impeccable Christ, and by His obedience He provided a righteousness without which man can never approach God (Rom. 10:1-4). Christ's Headship over man involved essence as well as office. There is a fullness in Christ which is absolutely impossible in depraved man (John 1:14,16; Col. 2:9). No man can be reverenced, but redeemed man's Head can be worshipped in the power of the Spirit.

The Headship of Christ is introduced by redemption. Christ has come in where there was nothing but chaos caused by the fall of Adam. He came to provide redemption for the lost sheep. The purpose of Christ could not be frustrated; He came to *seek and save the lost.* The gospel of redemption is not a gospel of possibility but *certainty.* Therefore, the recipients of redemption acknowledge Christ their Head with reverence.

Holding on to Christ as Head is the prize of the Christian's heart. *"Let no man beguile you of your reward* in a voluntary humility and worshipping of angels, intruding into those things which he hath not seen, vainly puffed up by his fleshly mind, *And not holding the Head,* from which all the body by joints and bands having nourishment ministered, and knit together, increaseth with the increase of God" (Col. 2:18,19). Holding the Head means that Christ is the Object of the saint's affection (Col. 3:1-3). False humility, leaning on false mediators, and intellectual self-conceit are certain to keep a person away from Christ. Paul earnestly admonishes the Colossians because there is a race to be run and " ... he that endureth to the end shall be saved" (Matt. 10:22). The final test of reality in Christianity is *continuance.* "My mouth shall shew forth thy righteousness and thy salvation all the day; for I know not the numbers thereof. *I will go in the strength of the Lord God:* I will make mention of thy righteousness, even of thine only" (Ps. 71:15,16).

The truths which a person holds, and not some religious name he wears, constitute the firmness of his title. A person may give mental assent to certain objective facts, but he will not persevere unless he has had an inward experience of Grace. "They went out from us, but they were not of us; for if they had been of us, *they would no doubt have continued with us:* but they went out, that they might be made manifest that they were not all of us" (I John 2:19).

Perseverance in holding the Head is the manifestation of grace. When we speak of God's preservation and the saint's perseverance, we do not mean there is a convergence of preservation and perseverance. This would be equivalent to calling justification an act of God and sanctification an act of man. Perseverance is not a supplement to preservation; it only points to God's preservation. God's preservation, therefore, does not emanate from the believer's perseverance; but the saint's perseverance is the fruit of God's preservation (Ps. 138; Zech. 3; John 10; Rom. 8).

Perseverance has no affinity with antinomianism. Antinomianism is the theory that Christians are freed from the moral law by virtue of grace. No Biblically minded person denies that the Christian sins, but he affirms that the believer cannot abandon himself to sin. There is a difference between the sins of the saved and those of the unsaved. The Christian sins from weakness and returns to God by conversion; the unsaved person lives in sin and does not return to God by conversion because he has never been brought to God by regeneration. If someone wishes to stress that the sheep are given to Christ (John 10:29), he must also emphasize that these sheep *hear Christ's voice and they follow Him.* All the cry about "eternal security" is of no avail apart from perseverance. God uses the means of reverential fear to cause His people to persevere. " ... I will put my fear in their hearts, that they shall not depart from me" (Jer. 32:40). Perseverance is a doxology to God's preservation.

The Headship of Christ not only represents His sovereignty, but the metaphor points to Christ as the *source of spiritual life* in the Body of Christ. The life which flows from the Head is diffused through every member of the Body as the life-blood of the physical body feeds and sustains its every member. Saints are bound unto Christ by His Spirit as the members of the physical body are held together by bones, sinews, and skin.

The Impeccable Saviour is the source of unity. Many local churches have been bound together by other bonds such as creeds, polity, and programs; but the *external* bond is like a rope binding a bundle of dead branches from a tree. *Inward* unity which springs from common possession of life is like a tree through which the same sap circulates from the trunk to the smallest leaf at the tip of the farthest branch. Christians share a common spiritual life. They have all eaten the same spiritual meat and drunk the same spiritual drink (I Cor. 10:3,4). All saints possess a Divine relationship which draws them to each other with one accord. "And all that believed were *together ...* " (Acts 2:44). "And the multitude of them that believed were of *one heart and of one soul ...* " (Acts 4:32). "For by *one Spirit* are we all baptized into *one body,* whether we be Jews or Gentiles, whether we be bond or free; and *have been all made to drink into one Spirit*" (I Cor. 13:13).

Jesus Christ is Head of the Church. "And he (Christ) is the head of *the body, the church ...* " (Col. 1:18). The formation of this Body, of which Christ is the risen Head, is the workmanship of the

Spirit. *Body* is never used in the plural form in the New Testament. Christ's Body is one, but it consists of many members. *Body (soma)* and *Church (ekklesia)* are both singular in this verse and refer to the mystical (spiritual) Body, the Church.

Christ builds the Church of which He is Head. "And I say also unto thee, That thou art Peter, and upon this rock *I will build my church;* and the gates of hell shall not prevail against it" (Matt. 16:18). Our Lord was speaking to the *local assembly* of disciples. He told the local assembly that *He would build His Church* which would constitute His spiritual Body. When the word Church is used in this sense, it emphasizes two things: (1) All who belong to this assembly are truly saved, and (2) The company of saints are distinguished from all branches of organized religion. Christ Jesus is the sovereign Lord Who rules over all, but He is Head only of the spiritual Body (Eph. 1:22,23).

The word church, unlike the word Body, is used in both a visible (local) and invisible (mystical) sense. For example, to be a church it need not be a continual assembly. The assembly is an assembly even when it is not assembled. The members who are providentially hindered from some of the local gatherings remain members; this constitutes an assembly within an assembly. Even a local church is invisible, as far as the local gathering is concerned, when it is not assembled.

Spiritually, the Church is one and can never be divided; *physically,* its members are scattered throughout the world. Some members of Christ's Body are already with Him, but they are waiting for the resurrection of their bodies. Many are on the earth at the present time, but they are separated from each other by great distances. There are some yet unborn who shall constitute a portion of the Church which Christ Jesus is building. This does not mean, however, that all can never be assembled together in one place at one time. "That in the dispensation of the fulness of times he (Christ) might *gather together in one all things in Christ,* both which are in heaven, and which are on earth; even in him" (Eph. 1:10). What a glorious assembly meeting this will be!

The importance of the Body of Christ must not be minimized. A serious error results when the Body of Christ is reduced to a local assembly containing both saved and unsaved. The Biblical view of the Body of Christ destroys institutional idolatry. Man-made institutions are claiming authority which God never delegated to them. Salvation is not in the hands of denominationally prejudiced people, but in the hands of Him Who saves whom He will and adds to His Church (John 1:11-13; Acts 2:41-47). The most important question which man faces is not to what denominational institution he belongs, but "What think ye of Christ?" (Matt. 22:42).

Local churches have valuable function in the purpose of God. They are not an end in themselves, but a means to an end. They exist for the sake of Christ's Body. Here the invisible finds expression as the soul of man finds expression in his body. As Paul did not neglect his duties in the local churches because he was a member of the invisible Body of Christ (II Tim. 4:1-8), so neither do informed Christians today. The Gospel has been committed to local churches for propagation. The purpose of the local church is not to socialize.

The local church is reproached in our day by institutional religion for failure to participate in temporal interests, intellectual progress, and social reform. She readily admits that this is not her mission; she points to something higher than that which is temporal, wiser than intellectual progress of natural man, and to a society for the Lord instead of against Him. A valuable lesson can be learned from Christ's refusal to be drawn into a social problem. "And one of the company said unto him, Master, speak to my brother, that he divide the inheritance with me. And he said unto him, Man, who made me a judge or a divider over you" (Luke 12:13,14). The Lord was showing that His mission was not to socialize mankind, but to redeem the elect. He disclaimed the position of Judge or Divider, but did show that the person who spoke was as guilty of covetousness as the one he blamed. Christ would not take from the oppressor and give to the oppressed, much less to encourage the oppressed to take from the oppressor. Our Lord forbade oppression.

Jesus Christ did not commit His truth to institutional religions, but to local churches. The value of the local church is emphasized by the fact she is locally governed. In institutional religions, however, local societies are governed by the hierarchy. When the hierarchy becomes corrupt, the whole system is corrupted. But when the government is in the hands of each local church, when one church becomes corrupt like Laodicea, the others are not infected. The others are in a position to quarantine the infected church to prevent the spread of her heresy into their midst. The principle of separation must not be ignored by God's people (II Cor. 6:14-18; Heb. 13:13). The testimony of God's people is found in the language of the Psalmist, "I am a companion of all them that fear thee, and of them that keep thy precepts" (Ps. 119:63).

Did Christ commit the *keys of the Kingdom of heaven* to the local church? The Lord Jesus was not speaking about the local church when He gave the promise of the keys. It was the Church against which the gates of hell should never prevail. No local church can lay claim to that promise. The most spiritual and orthodox church can never say that Satan has not made some inroad into her midst. There is no guarantee of the perpetuity of the local church because the candlestick may be removed, but the Church which is Christ's Body will prevail because her perpetuity is guaranteed.

Authority given to the Church is to be exercised in the Kingdom of heaven. According to the context, this Kingdom will have been established on the earth (Matt. 16:27-17:13). The Kingdom and reign of the saints are said to be in the future. A tragic mistake is made by interpreters of Scripture when they identify the keys of the Kingdom with the authority of the local or institutional church. Such teaching has been the source of great evil; a totalitarian spirit has been derived from such false concept of authority and is felt in every institutional or local church that embraces this idea. Such authority could never be given even to redeemed men because they are imperfect. This authority is given to the Body of Christ (the redeemed of the Lord) and will be exercised when they shall reign with Christ in the Kingdom (Rev. 5:10). This denotes perfection.

The local church is not to be designated by the name of some person, creed, polity, or ordinance; she is designated by her geographical location (I Cor. 1:2; Eph. 1:1; Phil. 1:1; Col. 1:2; Rev. 1:11). God's people are designated by the names which include all saints such as believers, saints, brethren, children of God, disciples, and Christians (Acts 5:14; Phil. 1:1; II Thess. 1:3; John 11:52; Acts 20:7; Acts 11:26). Jesus Christ is the center for drawing Christians together. How sad to see people drawn together by creeds and programs rather than the Person and Work of Christ.

Christ's Headship is viewed in connection with the Bride (Eph. 5:22-33). There are two wonderful types of the Bride in the Old Testament. They are Eve and Rebekah. God's sovereignty is manifested in Eve; the practical effect of the Spirit is revealed in Rebekah. Eve was passive; it was all God's work typified in regeneration. The experimental side of regeneration is shown in Rebekah. The thoughts of her heart were exercised by the servant's testimony concerning Isaac. Does not the Lord have the sovereign right to choose His Bride? Arminianism presents Christ as a Person Who will marry anyone who will have Him, but this is not the gospel of the Bible.

The Headship of Christ demonstrates the true form of church government. Both undershepherds and Christians are to be submissive to Jesus Christ because of their love for Him. Local churches have their ministers who watch out for the souls of the redeemed (Heb. 13:17; Acts 20:28). They are responsible to Christ, not the people, to Whom they must give account. Ministers are not men pleasers; those who please men are not the servants of Christ (Gal. 1:10). Saints are to submit themselves to the laws of Christ which are executed by God's ministers. Their submission issues from love to Christ; not from love to Christ's ministers. God's servants are held in high esteem for their work's sake (I Thess. 5:12,13). The church, therefore, is not a democracy in which rule is from beneath; *she is a theocracy because she is ruled from above by Him Who is her only Head.*

CHRIST'S KINGSHIP

The perfection of Christ's work on Calvary will be consummated in the Kingdom. The consummation of His work is not to be understood as including any additional redemptive work because that is contrary to the one perfect sacrifice for sin. "For by one offering he (Christ) hath perfected for ever them that are sanctified" (Heb. 10:14). No Christian will say that his salvation, which had its beginning in regeneration, is complete. This is the reason he groans within himself, waiting for the redemption of the body (Rom. 8:23). The perfection of a Christian's salvation will be finished in the glorification of his body (I John 3:2,3). Thus, the totality of salvation will have its completion at Christ's second advent. "So Christ was once offered to bear the sins of many; and unto them that look for him shall he appear the second time without sin *unto salvation*" (Heb. 9:28).

Salvation of the Christian is often referred to as taking place in the future. " ... Lo, this is our God; we have waited for him, and he will save us: this is the Lord; we have waited for him, we will be glad and rejoice in his salvation" (Is. 25:9). God's people never wait in vain. Israel is preserved through all her time of waiting, and now in prophesy Isaiah sees the time of her deliverance. "Rejoice ye with Jerusalem, and be glad with her, all ye that love her: rejoice for joy with her ... Behold, I will extend peace to her like a river ... " (Is. 66:10,12). Paul said to the Roman Christians, " ... for now is our salvation nearer than when we believed" (Rom. 13:11). The Roman saints were admonished to be more diligent in their Christian life since the end of their race was nearer than when they started. As the man in a race runs harder as he nears the finish mark, so the Christian should have a deeper concern for the will of God as he approaches the end of his earthly pilgrimage. Rivers have more depth and force as they near the ocean than when they began in some small mountain stream. Solomon said, " ... the path of the just is as the shining light, that shineth more and more unto the perfect day" (Prov. 4:18).

The just have a path in which they run their race. This path is entered by the gateway of justification; the justified persons are maintained in their path by sanctification to its goal, glorification.

God *declares* the repentant believer justified on the ground of the substitutionary work of Christ. *"Being justified freely by his grace through the redemption that is in Christ Jesus:* Whom God hath set forth to be a propitiation *through faith* in his blood, to declare his righteousness for the remission of sins that are past, through the forbearance of God"* (Rom. 3:24,25). Jesus Christ is a propitiation *through faith;* not to those who have no faith. *Through faith* does not mean by faith; faith is not the ground of justification. The *originating cause* of justification is grace; the *effectual cause* is Christ's redemptive death; the *means is through faith.* Justification is by God (Rom. 8:33) ; not by faith. Too many people make a god out of their faith. The merit is not in faith, but in the Object of faith. The Person and work of Jesus Christ is the Object of justifying faith. Christ's Impeccable Life of representative law-keeping obtained the righteousness for His own sheep, and His redemptive death bore the punishment of His people's sins.

Sanctification, unlike justification, is something God has done *in the repentant believer.* It has been said that guilt, penalty, and stain proceed from sin. Christ's death has removed the penalty for His people; His satisfaction removed the guilt; His sanctification removes the stain. Penalty and guilt are out of the question for the Christian, but he is often overwhelmed by his consciousness of stain. "Having therefore these promises, dearly beloved, let us cleanse ourselves from all filthiness of the flesh and spirit, perfecting holiness in the fear of God" (II Cor. 7:1). Sanctification, therefore, is both absolute and progressive. The change that took place in regeneration is *absolute,* but the change that started in regeneration will be reflected in many *progressive* changes until the final change.

Glorification is the final change in the Christian. This is the goal to which all things are moving. What is the hope of the Christian? It is not deliverance *from* the body, but deliverance *of* the body in resurrection power. Death is an alarming subject even to the Christian; however, the second coming of Christ is a glorious subject to the saint because it means to be like Christ. The first coming of Christ brought saving grace, but the second advent perfects it; Christ's first coming brought the earnest of redemption in humiliation, but the second coming perfects it in glory.

The Kingdom means many things to many people, but *there is one positive Biblical interpretation.* The Kingdom is not the Church, either visible or invisible. It is neither soteriological nor providential; the Kingdom is eschatological and is connected with the second advent of Jesus Christ. Just as the perfection of Christ's human nature cannot be denied, neither can the perfection of His work which finds its consummation in the Kingdom.

As theocracy (rule from above) is the only true form of church government, so the theocratic rule of Christ in the Kingdom is the only true form of world government. There are many forms of human government, but they will all prove to be a failure before the government of the world shall rest upon the shoulder of Jesus Christ (Is. 9:6). Human government, like every thing administered by men, must be imperfect. There is no such thing as absolute human justice, and there never will be a perfect form of human government administered by imperfect men.

All the powers of men are ordained of God. Paul said, " ... For there is no power but of God: the powers that be are ordained of God" (Rom. 13:1). Some form of human government, as imperfect as it might be, is needed. This is to prevent complete anarchy. Obedience to such authority is demanded, but not when God's law is violated (Acts 4:19; 5:29). Our submission to existing powers does not mean that the *character* of that government is acceptable to God. A power that God orders can be, as far as its character is concerned, described as a dreadful beast. "And the ten horns which thou sawest upon *the beast,* these shall hate the whore, and shall make her desolate and naked, and shall eat her flesh, and burn her with fire. For *God hath put in their hearts to fulfill his will,* and to agree, and *give their kingdom unto the beast,* until the words of God shall be fulfilled" (Rev. 17:16,17). This verse demonstrates the way God disposes of kingdoms and appoints rulers according to His sovereign pleasure. The imperfect government of men causes the Christian to long for the perfect Kingdom of Christ.

We do not have to study Euclid, the Greek educator, to know that *the whole is greater than the part.* Some eschatologists seem to believe that the part is greater than the whole because they say the proper interpretation of the Kingdom is spiritual and has no reference to the future visible Kingdom on earth. But how can the Lord Jesus be in possession of that which He has gone to receive from the Father? When received, He will return to establish His reign over all the world (Luke 19:11-27). This will be the crowning consummation of His work.

There are three things to be observed in the parable by our Lord in Luke 19. (1) The Kingdom for which some looked would not appear at that time. ". . . they thought that the kingdom of God should immediately appear" (Luke 19:11). (2) The period of time between Christ's return to the Father and His second advent is occupied with calling the elect by the proclamation of the Gospel. Christians become *heirs* of the Kingdom (James 2:5), but the realization thereof awaits the manifestation of the Kingdom. They are to walk worthy of God Who has called them *unto* His Kingdom (I Thess. 2:12). (3) Christ's second coming will be in power and glory. "When the Son of Man shall come in his glory, and all the holy angels with him, then shall He sit upon the throne of his glory" (Matt. 25:31). The Lord Jesus is now being honored in heaven after His redemptive work on the cross. This honor, which Christ is receiving at the Father's right hand, will be manifested in the very place where He has been dishonored.

The Kingdom is not to be confused with Christ's sovereign rule. His sovereignty is never associated with promise; this is eternally His by virtue of His Deity. The Kingdom, however, belongs to Jesus Christ as the "Son of David" and the "Son of Man"; and this is connected with promise. As the Son of God, Christ is ever with the Father; but as the Son of Man (the God-Man), He manifests Himself (and the Father through Him) on earth in the hypostatic union adapted to redeemed mankind.

Is it materialistic to believe in a literal Kingdom on earth? This is the accusation many religionists bring against Christians who believe in the future Kingdom of Christ on earth. Such accusation is a reflection against the Person of the Son of Man. Was Christ materialistic when in humanity He suffered and died? Is it not true that humanity itself was adorned by such relationship? In the Impeccable human nature of Christ, we have the embodiment of sinlessness and truth. This relationship is a guarantee that our Lord will not stop with the salvation of the soul. He will redeem the body and then the earth on which His fullest glory shall be displayed in His Kingdom which shall never end. To Christ be all the praise, honor, and glory both now and forever!